# Health and Physical Education of Young Children

International Society of Physical Education of Young Children
President Dr. Akira MAEHASHI
(Waseda University, Professor/Doctor of Medicine)

**University Education Press**

# Preface

In early childhood education, Physical Education activities are often used to promote better physical and mental development of children. Playing all kinds of sports and sport games plays an important role in experience accumulation for enhancing both physical and mental development. In short, "Physical Education of Young Children" is needed to educate children and parents for having sufficient physical activities. This does not only let children learn about various movements, but this also helps improve children's cardio-pulmonary function, skeletal development and physical fitness. Moreover, this helps children develop self-protection awareness as well. Consequently, all these promote a positive effect on lifelong physical fitness and health, cultivate a positive and caring spirit, promote a stable mood and stimulate creative abilities. Therefore, we can see that Physical Education always lays a good foundation that will allow children to experience a rich and fulfilling life.

Since "Physical Education of Young Children" has

important significance in children's daily lives, our IPEC Society endeavors to promote better "Physical Education of Young Children" all over the world, applying theories into practical use. We work as a team to actively promote better Physical Education for Young Children. Please pay close attention to our Society and come to join us if you agree with our objectives. Our team is enthusiastic about Physical Education of Young Children and we hope that you can help us in our research work and support our activities to promote a better future for young children.

>International Society of Physical Education of Young Children (IPEC)
>President　Dr. Akira Maehashi

Health and Physical Education
of Young Children

## Contents

Preface .................................................................................... i

---
## Part 1  Theory
---

**Chapter 1**
Daily rhythm improvement strategy: Encouraging
the "Eat, be active and sleep well" movement ............... *3*

   1. Three problems faced by children in recent years ......... *3*
      (1) Sleep rhythm out of order   *3*
      (2) Eating rhythm out of order   *4*
      (3) Lack of exercise   *5*

   2. Body temperature rhythm affected by the autonomic
      nerves and hormones in the brain ................................. *6*

   3. Launch of the "Go to bed early, get up early and have
      breakfast" movement and challenges ............................ *9*

   4. The importance in meeting new challenges ................... *11*

**Chapter 2**
Why are physical activities during young childhood
so important? ............................................................... *13*

   1. The problem is not just about physical activities ............ *13*
   2. Impressing experience forms "Liking" ........................... *15*
   3. It will even help enough just by watching over ............. *16*
   4. Society, life cycle, and children's bodies corresponded
      coaching to the various changes .................................... *18*

## Chapter 3
### Significance and charm of "the physical education of young children" ··················································· 20

1. Position statement for the physical education of young children ··················································· 21
2. About physical education ································· 22
3. Aim of the physical education ···························· 23
4. The ways of the physical education ····················· 24
5. Exercise as an infant experience it ····················· 26
6. Points to keep in mind when instructing physical education of young children instruction ·················· 27
7. The instruction method of the physical education program ································································· 30
8. End ································································· 33

## Chapter 4
### Suggestions for physical education instruction methods for young children ··················································· 34

1. Noteworthy points at the introductory scene ············ 34
   (1) Safe environmental setting  *34*
   (2) Clothing  *35*
   (3) Teacher's standing position  *36*
   (4) Formation  *37*
   (5) Alignment  distance to children  *38*
   (6) Warm-up  *39*
   (7) Grouping  *40*
2. Noteworthy points at the development scene ············ 40
   (1) Manner of speaking  *40*

(2) Consideration for the fearsome children  *41*
(3) Momentum  *41*
(4) Assistance  *42*
(5) Mastering skills  *42*
(6) Sustained concentration  *43*
(7) The making of a pleasant atmosphere  *44*
(8) Feeling of satisfaction  *44*
(9) Stirring up motivation  *45*
(10) Fostering independence, spontaneity and creativity  *45*
(11) Response to danger  *47*
(12) Competition  *47*

3. Ending scene ················································································ *47*
(1) Cooling down exercise  *47*
(2) Clearing  *48*
(3) Summary of the activity  *49*
(4) Security after the exercise and hygiene  *49*

## Chapter 5
Park play equipment and raising children ·························· *50*

Introduction ···························································································· *50*

1. Health management problems experienced by
   children in recent years ······························································· *51*
   (1) Negative influence on children by pursuing an adult nightlife  *51*
   (2) Negative impact of excessive media contact on children  *54*

2. How to increase the work of children's brain and
   autonomic nerves ············································································ *57*

3. Significance and role of park play equipment ················ *59*
   (1) Slide stand  *60*

(2) Swing　　*61*
  
  (3) Monkey bars　　*61*
  
  (4) Monument playground equipment: dinosaur play equipment　　*61*
  
  (5) Tree climbing playground equipment　　*62*

4. Ability to be cultivated with park playground equipment ·················································································· *63*

  (1) 10 physical fitness factors　　*63*
  
  (2) 4Basic movement skills　　*66*
  
  (3) Ability to grow during exercise　　*67*
  
  (4) Safety management (basic) of park playground equipment and safe usage　　*68*

---

## Part 2　Movement Activities

## Chapter 1
## Children's enjoyable exercise and sports festival events ······················································· *75*

1. Warming-up ················································································· *75*

  (1) Warming up　　*76*
  
  (2) Changing postures　　*76*
  
  (3) Jumping up of Ninja　　*77*
  
  (4) Opening, closing, closing　　*77*
  
  (5) Standing up back to back　　*77*
  
  (6) Mushroom gymnastics　　*78*

2. Exercising in pairs ······································································ *78*

  (1) Clap and tap　　*78*
  
  (2) Rock-paper-scissors: hitting hands　　*79*
  
  (3) Rock-paper-scissors: one circle of the world　　*79*

     (4) Rock-paper-scissors: drilling through battock   *80*
     (5) Taking tails   *80*

3. Exercise involving adults and children ·························· *81*
     (1) Jumping across feet and going around   *81*
     (2) Jumping and tunneling   *82*
     (3) Jumping and closing feet   *83*
     (4) Foot race in the air   *83*
     (5) Sumo of crouching down   *84*
     (6) Race to step on someone's foot   *85*
     (7) Patting someone on the butt (using towel)   *85*
     (8) Laying logs   *86*
     (9) Push-ups and shaking hands   *87*
     (10) Wheelbarrow → shaking hands with children who met → somersault   *88*
     (11) Pull towel   *88*

4. Exercise games using wood reuse ····························· *89*
     (1) Paper runner (newspaper)   *89*
     (2) Making balls of newspaper (newspaper: 2Sheets)   *89*
     (3) Catching balls of newspaper (newspaper)   *90*
     (4) Volleyball of a plastic shopping bag (plastic shopping bag)   *90*
     (5) Catch air balls made from plastic shopping bags (plastic shopping bag part 2)   *91*
     (6) Play a game of catching with an apron (apron, newspaper)   *91*
     (7) Play a game of catching balls with a container (detergent case, milk bottle)   *92*

5. Sports day games ·········································· *92*
     (1) Torch relay   *92*
     (2) Pass through between legs and compete   *93*

Contents  ix

 (3) Hold hands, fold back and compete *93*
 (4) Express courier service of kangaroo
   (game of carrying balls) *94*
 (5) Rolling peanuts balls *95*
 (6) Opening legs' race/laying race/putting feet
   up race *96*
 (7) Laying, setting up, and carrying
   (obstacle race involving parent and child) *97*
 (8) Carrying shooters by small radius *97*
 (9) Safe driving everyday (race blindfold) *98*
 (10) Busy loop (race to pass hula-hoop) *99*
 (11) Magic carpet *99*
 (12) Two people as one and cooperate *100*
 (13) Surfing of sea otters *100*
 (14) Cutting waves of flying fish (four flying fish) *101*
 (15) Taking tails against other teams *102*
 (16) Go! Go! Hurricane
   (race to carry bars → race to pass hula-hoop) *102*

## Chapter 2
## Exercises using familiar items ·········· *104*

 1. Play to put towels ············································· *105*

 2. Play to take towels ············································ *106*

 3. Catching plastic bags········································· *108*

 4. Kicking valley of plastic shopping bags ················ *109*

 5. Taking tails ······················································ *110*

 6. Race to roll balls by rackets ······························· *112*

 7. T-ball play: running around circle ······················ *113*

 8. T-ball play: ball collectors ·································· *116*

## Chapter 3
Rhythm/Expression ················································· 119

  1. Circle dance ················································· 119

  2. The choo-choo train in flowerland ······················ 123

  3. Warm warm walk walk ···································· 127

  4. Bright red sun ················································ 132

## Chapter 4
Playing games of tags ············································· 137

  1. Playing fantastic games of tags can
   nurture children's mind. ·································· 137

  2. Variations are infinity depending on twists
   and ideas ························································ 138

  3. Step-up of playing games of tags ······················· 138

  4. Producing "Champions" ···································· 139

  5. "One tag" ······················································· 139
    (1) Waving tag    *139*
    (2) Stepping tag    *141*
    (3) Coloring tag    *142*
    (4) Baby chicks and a cat    *144*
    (5) Dropping the handkerchief game    *145*

  6. Collecting tags ················································ 146
    (1) Collecting tags    *146*
    (2) Collecting tags' team    *148*
    (3) Catching fish    *149*

  7. Increasing tags ··············································· 150
    (1) Holding hands tags    *150*

(2) Pulling tags  *152*

8. Helping tags ·················································· *153*
   (1) Freezing tags  *154*
   (2) Kick-the-can  *156*

**Profile of the author** ······································· *158*

The Administration Staff ········································· *160*

The Consultant Staff ············································· *161*

Instructor Training Committee ···································· *162*

Japanese Society of Physical Education of Young
Children, Professional Instructors ································ *164*

Editorial Board ··················································· *166*

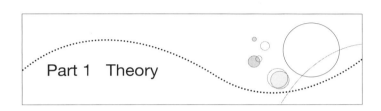

# Part 1  Theory

# Daily rhythm improvement strategy: Encouraging the "Eat, be active and sleep well" movement

## 1. Three problems faced by children in recent years

### (1) Sleep rhythm out of order

The first concern is that more and more children in today's Japanese society are becoming night owls. It is now a common sight to see children brought to family restaurants, pubs, karaoke bars, etc. by their parents late at night. Some pubs have even begun to provide designated areas and special menus for children. In fact, growing numbers of parents are letting their children stay up late, saying things like "No problem. Our children are full of life", "Night is the time when children can have quality time with their father" or "Our children say they are not sleepy yet". Consequently, today's children increasingly tend to "go to bed late, wake up late and always feel tired!" The fact that more than 40% of Japanese young children go to bed after 10p.m. is a national crisis in Japan. The problems here are "lack of knowledge" and "low awareness," causing parents to be ignorant about healthy lifestyles for their children and preventing them from helping their children maintain natural daily rhythms, as well as the nocturnal lifestyles of many adults, all these lead their children into unhealthy lifestyles. So, what actually happens when young children do not sleep long enough (ten hours) at night? These children, particularly short-sleeping ones who sleep fewer than nine and a half hours, tend to demonstrate behavioral characteristics, such as being less able to exercise caution or concentrate, easily becoming irritated, or being hyperactive and constantly on the move. Such children can neither keep their composure nor properly take part in kindergarten activities, and are likely to have trouble focusing on their lessons after moving on to elementary school.

### (2) Eating rhythm out of order

When children go to bed late at night and wake up late in the morning, they are lacking of sleep and often fail to have a full breakfast or even skip breakfast alltogether. This is the second concern. Skipping breakfast can make children irritable and cause young children to demonstrate behaviors such as throwing building blocks, treating their toys roughly and suddenly hitting friends from behind. Today, however, only 80% of Japanese young children have breakfast every morning. At the same time, increasing numbers of children are failing to have bowel movements at home to make a fresh start in the morning before arriving at kindergarten, resulting in many children not showing up in good spirits. When this is the case, it is no wonder that more children become less active in the morning. Reduced physical activities lead to a decline in the daily amount of exercise and prevent children from appropriately building up their physical strength.

### (3) Lack of exercise

The third concern is that there has been a marked decrease in the amount of exercise taken by children in their daily lives. For example, the number of steps walked by an average five-year-old nursery school child from 9:00 a.m. to 4:00 p.m., which was about 12,000 in 1985〜1987, dropped to 7,000〜8,000 in 1991〜1993. The number fell below 5,000 after 1998 and the current amount of physical activites done by young children has become less than half compared to the Showa period (1926〜89). In addition, as it has become more common for children to commute between home and school by car, there has been a decline in the total number of steps walked by children during the whole day. This results in a lack of exercise which is essential for children to build up their physical strength.

## 2. Body temperature rhythm affected by the autonomic nerves and hormones in the brain

Staying awake until hours can disturb the sleep rhythms of children, which in turn, can interrupt their eating rhythms, leading to no breakfast and no defecation. The result of this can be reduced physical activities in the morning, affected by morning sleepiness and fatigue. This can cause not only a decrease in their physical strength, but also impaired functioning of the autonomic nerves, which can upset their day-and-night body temperature rhythms (Figure 1).

This is the reason why there are children with "hyperthermia" and "hypothermia," whose core body temperatures are not maintained at a stable 36℃ level since they cannot control their body temperatures. In addition, when nocturnal children whose body temperature rhythms are disturbed, they are inactive in the morning with a low body temperature and become active at night with a high body temperature.

Generally speaking, human body temperature maintains a certain cycle in daily lives in which it becomes lowest at around 3:00a.m. at night and highest at around 4:00p.m. in the afternoon, influenced by hormones in the brain (Figure 2). This circadian variability is one of the biological rhythms that human beings have acquired over time. For example, around 4:00p.m. in the afternoon is the time of the day when people become most active.

This is why I call it children's "Golden Time for Playing and Learning." I believe it should be the time of the day in which children should exercise their curiosity and look for things that catch their interests, for example nature, animals, sports games, chidren should enjoy playing as much as they can. By experiencing such enthusiasm, attempting new things and repeating a cycle of creating ideas and putting them into practice, over and over again, children can achieve dramatic growth.

However, the body temperature rhythms of children who lead nocturnal lifestyles are several hours behind the normal body temperature rhythm. Their bodies are not really awake and are still inactive in the morning,

> Keeping late hours can interrupt the sleep rhythms of chidren.
> ↓
> Disturbed eating rhythms (No breakfast)
> ↓
> Declines in physical activities in the morning and daily amounts of exercise
> (Lack of exercise and weakened physical strength)
> ↓
> Impaired functioning of the autonomic nerves that automatically protect the human body (Upset day-and-night body temperature rhythms, interfering with autonomous, voluntary behaviors)
> ↓
> Interrupted hormone secretion rhythms
> (Difficulty in waking up in the morning, inactivity during the day, and inability to get a good night's sleep)
> ↓
> Higher risk of physical and mental instability
> ↓
> Deterioration of academic performance, declining physical strength, truancy, violence

Figure 1  The flow and onset of problems common to Japanese children

as they have to get up and start the day while their body temperatures are still as low as when they are asleep. The reverse is also true; their body temperatures remain high at night, causing them to have difficulty in falling asleep and leading to a vicious cycle. Restoring these delayed body temperature rhythms back to normal is the key to the success of the daily

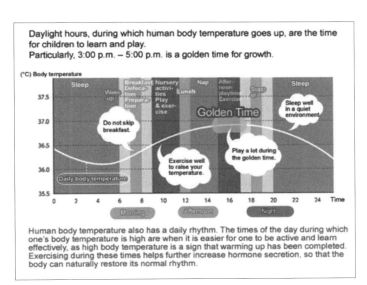

Figure 2  Daily body temperature rhythm

rhythm improvement strategy. Here are the two most effective methods of achieving this end: (1) exposing children to sunshine in the morning and (2) getting them to exercise during the day.

## 3. Launch of the "Go to bed early, get up early and have breakfast" movement and challenges

Put simply, the solution to the problems experienced by children is to get adults to take more seriously about the "lifestyles that babies, toddlers and children should have (to achieve a good dietary, exercise and rest balance)." In fact, the "Go to bed early, get up early and have breakfast" movement is a nationwide movement that Japan has developed as the result of its efforts to achieve the above. Although this movement is very effective in encouraging people to take action to promote health, we must admit that there is still room for improvement before it can bring more vitality to children by proactively stimulating their autonomic nervous systems.

Figure 1 illustrates my view of how problems faced by Japanese children have developed. If you want to stop these problems from continuing, the first thing to do is to take "sleep" more seriously to help protect and nurture the brains of children. This is why I emphasize the importance of "going to bed early and getting up early". Another important thing is to place special emphasis on "breakfast," as sleep disorders lead to "eating" disorders.

A shortcoming of this nationwide movement, however, is that it only covers these two aspects, while the third one, "Exercise," should also be an indispensable part of the daily lives of children, if you expect them to become self-motivated, self-directed and able to think and act independently. In fact, exercise and physical play are essential for the development of autonomic functions. It is necessary, also from the perspective of lifestyle improvement, that we should not overlook the importance of providing children with opportunities and occasions, as part of their daily lives, to take exercise during the day to let out their physical energy and release their emotions.

To this end, it is essential that another element, "Exercise," should be added to the nationwide "Go to bed early, get up early and have breakfast" movement. To put it plainly, it should be "Eat, be active and sleep well." In other words, the key is to launch a campaign that emphasizes the importance of "physical activity" and proactively put it into practice. My wish is that children, who are afterall our future, can develop healthy lifestyles and lead healthy, fulfilling lives.

## 4. The importance in meeting new challenges

What is crucial for children now? A new challenge is to introduce the importance of "Exercise" into the campaign. The "Eat well, Move well and Sleep well" campaign through the concerted efforts of kindergartens and nurseries with the families and the local authorities, can be implemented nation-wide. It is time that we all join and get involved.

Sports (exercise) and sporting games do not just make one stronger, it improves metabolism, body temperature control and plays an important role in brain or nerve system functions too. It is important that the kindergartens and nurseries, schools and local authorities ensure an environment conducive to sport play where children can play fully engrossed and forget about time – this will help them grow safely. For the sake of a healthy future for our children, it is important for the society and all adults to work together single-mindedly to provide a good environment for sports and make exercise a part of our daily lives. Let's contribute our hearty efforts to make the world a happy place for our children to grow up in.

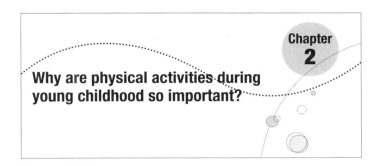

## Chapter 2
## Why are physical activities during young childhood so important?

### 1. The problem is not just about physical activities

"The decline in scholastic ability", "the decline in physical strength" and "mental problems." have become important issues. Why did these three issues appear for Japanese children to handle in recent years? When we think it over, we can see the problems are stemming from life cycle deficiencies. The society as a whole is becoming a "night person" society, which is making normal sleep cycles impossible. This leads eating cycles going wrong and so on. When the eating cycles are disrupted and children do not take breakfast, they cannot store enough energy to complete normal activities, and they also lose concentration skills easily. More over, a hungry child loses patience quickly. In these conditions, it is obvious that normal vitality declines. Usually, a body gets tired and then gains strength through activities, this is how human beings gain physical strength. When there are no chances, the physical strength declines. Moreover, rest (sleeping), nutrition (eating), physical activities (playing) make up one day cycle. When the cycle balance breaks, the brain and autonomic nerves, which protect your body, start to work improperly. When this escalates, the hormone balance, which keeps the body temperature, goes wrong. As a result, daily physical conditioning deteriorates, mental function become unstable and this leads to "the decline in scholastic ability", "the decline in physical strength" and "school refusal."

These culminate in problems of the mind and body. Today, we have started to figure out that these problems about life cycles do not only influence physical strength and physical knowledge, but it also influences mental development. Therefore, when we need to think about "physical activities," we need to look at the whole life cycle, and discuss a better exercise program in detail and the better way of coaching. Young childhood is the time when the brain and the nervous system develop. So, to firmly establish healthy life habits such as sleeping and eating habits, and to promote the growth of physical movements and physical knowledge, we must help children build these habits when they are young. Keeping this in mind, let's get to work.

## 2. Impressing experience forms "Liking"

During young childhood, the time when the base of the ability, to form physical knowledge is made, we experience many movements. It is important for children to feel "I want to do it, I want to play" with a positive will. By helping children develop this positive will, the movement they wanted to form, becomes diversified, and the movements they worked on by themselves improves during their mid-to-latter period of young childhood. Let's keep introducing many other movements, so that they will keep improving their movements. The experience like "yeah," feeling empowered, when children climb on the vaulting horse, will raise children's confidence to do even more. Please appraise children's movement to show the feeling of like "yeah," whether they were able to make or not. Those positive experiences will make them feel that they want to accomplish more new movements. On the other hand, if you keep appraising only the knowledge, and scold just because they cannot not make it right, this will make your children not like exercising. The negative response can make it difficult to fix the negative experience afterwards.

### 3. It will even help enough just by watching over

Then, how can we raise children's exercise confidence levels when children do not have any knowledgeable ability? There is no need to think hard. Just observing your children will help a lot. Children always ask you to "Look! Look!" no matter if they are able to perform the skill or not. When someone is looking, just watching makes children happy. Plus, if you cheer them by saying "Good job", this will make them feel "I want to try again". And again, they will come over and let you see it, even they are not able to perform the task. In these times, when they need contact with people, it greatly helps just by watching. We have measured how much they are moving by putting a pedometer on the children. During free playing for two hours from 9 o'clock to 11 o'clock, the pedometer measures about three thousands steps. When the play surroundings are set up more interestingly, the pedometer measures up to five thousands steps. When teachers play together with them, the pedometer measures up to over six thousands steps. In other words, when the teachers are with them, play with them, laugh with them, and promote a positive play experience, the pedometer will probably measure higher exercise and step levels. Whether the teachers have the requisite coaching technique or not, it is just a matter of whether teachers are watching the children or not.

With the number of children decreasing, and the society changing, we do not see children playing around the local area as much as before. In spite of that, just by saying "play freely," physical gain will never expand. So, this is the time when teachers become the leader, play and coach new physical games. This will lead to the children playing more, and will foster much more physical movement. With vitality and physical strength gains, children will naturally become vigorously more active. If it does not work, it means that the problems are the play settings and surroundings, as well as the teachers willingness to get involved. We need to face the problems sincerely, and think about what we should do.

## 4. Society, life cycle, and children's bodies corresponded coaching to the various changes

When one element goes wrong, the life cycle goes wrong. On the other hand On besides, when one element improves, the life cycle improves. When you want to fix the life cycle, exercise and playing are very effective. Problems with today's children are related to a lack of physical stimulus at an appropriate time during the day. At what time period and what kind of physical games should teachers provide? In addition, the behaviors of the adults who are involved in the physical games and what kind of "words" they use to motivate the children will become very important. We should never forget the point that the physical games will activate life itself. Previously, there was a time when it was thought that "health is health", "life is life", and "physical activity is physical activity" all different and separated things, but it is now time to think about the relationships. It is becoming important to see how many teachers are seeing the problems and what they are doing to fix the problems. How are the coaches, who are teaching young children's physical education, do they only think about the improvement of physical movements and physical strength, are they employing an already old-fashioned idea? How much do they understand about our changing society, life cycles, and children's bodies, and what can they do to coach corresponding to that change, that change is needed now.

To solve the various children's problems from the root, we should never neglect the life cycle, rest, nutrition, physical activities, and the teachers who can support the development of children are very necessary.

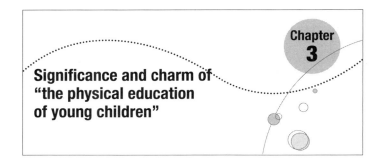

# Chapter 3

## Significance and charm of "the physical education of young children"

Hello, my name is Akira Maehashi. I studied adapted physical education and elementary physical education in the United States at the University of Missouri-Columbia and the University of Tennessee at Knoxville. I have continued my education and research at the University of Missouri and the University of Vermont in the United States, as well as, Kurashiki City College and Waseda University in Japan. Currently, I am expanding my research by communicating with physical educators from Korea, Taiwan, China, Philippines, Singapore, Germany, Finland, England, and the United States.

I believe that the physical education teachers from these countries have much in common, and will find value in learning from each other's experiences. I want to share the philosophies I have developed for physical educators who work with young children. Recently, I created a new organization "The International Society of Physical Education of Young Children" (IPEC) to bring these professionals together.

## 1. Position statement for the physical education of young children

My philosophy, when teaching physical education to young children, is to offer a variety of activities that develop movement skills naturally, in the interest of the children that are enjoyable, and encourage maximum participation. I believe in increasing the repetition of the movements rather than focusing on the technical improvement of the skills. When young children are motivated intrinsically, they will be more likely to be successful in their physical education experiences. Young children, who are not forced to improve, will develop a better sense of cooperation, respect, and enjoyment of exercise for a lifetime of fitness and good health.

## 2. About physical education

I think that physical education enhances the physical, social, intellectual, emotional, and spiritual aspects of human development through exercise play, movement games, sports play, rhythm, and dance. In a quality physical education program, young children develop a good balance of mind and body, with an emphasis on positive experiences in their exercise time and personal connections in their learning. Physical education should instill a love for movement and exercise that will lead to a lifetime of healthy habits for individuals as they age.

In addition, a structured curriculum is essential for a quality physical education program. Once the lessons are developed and practiced, teachers should examine their instruction methods and assess their effectiveness. Next, compare the progress and results with the intention of the lesson, and evaluate it for improvement. Make changes if necessary.

Above all, play with exercise and physical activity should be conducted with consideration of enjoyment, health promotion and safety management. Children begin to learn as infants through play. As babies grow, they learn to use their bodies to make discoveries.

They begin to reach and grasp, which allow them to explore in new ways. We guide their discoveries and teach them about their experiences as they occur, without much judgment or expectation to force learning. This is how most young children learn before they become kindergarten students. A quality physical education program for young children should continue to offer children similar learning experiences.

## 3. Aim of the physical education

What I value most in the instruction of the physical education of young children, is that the teacher should allow children to experience the joy of movement, so that it is "learned with heart." When young children have positive experiences in their physical education classes, the improvement of their physical strength and exercise skill will come through repeated practice of the exercises. In other words, I want to suggest, "change a heart through movement."

I believe that the physical education of young children should aim at three points:

① Respect self: think independently, recognize strengths and weaknesses, and act accordingly with one's own volition.

② Respect others: encourage rich human nature with a compassionate heart, be considerate to friends, and strive to please.
③ Respect health: practice the physical strength and exercise skills which can enhance a healthy lifestyle and improve the motor capability, safely.

## 4. The ways of the physical education

- Offer many experiences of various exercises through play, instead of carrying out a specific activity, aiming at only the improvement of the technical aspect. Allow children time to get used to exercise and various movements through play and enjoyment.
- Let children experience a variety of movements and feel the joy in advancing, moving and playing. Share your favorite exercises, activities, and experiences you enjoyed as a child.
- Let children acquire the pleasure and the joy of exercise by allowing them to work at their pace. Encourage them to work hard and guide their learning through repetition, similar to how we work with an infant's development.
- Strive for the improvement of children's strength for handling their body skillfully.

- Allow children time to make sense from their experiences as they did when learning as infants. They have been learning in this manner since they were small babies.
- Encourage children to use the wide variety of skills they developed in physical education classes and apply them in specific activities or sequences.
- Infants fall down often, usually without much problem or concern. They love to run and jump, and enjoy playing outdoors where they get dirty with soil. This love of play should be encouraged in physical education too.
- Increase opportunities for outdoor exercise experiences under natural settings.
- Happy children will value, and take responsibility for, engagement in physical activities for life.
- Children should have a basic knowledge about nutrition and a healthy balanced diet.
- Children should know the benefits of exercise and have an understanding of good postures.
- Develop children's eagerness to learn through exercise play, to gain pleasure, and satisfaction.

## 5. Exercise as an infant experiences it

I feel that physical education of young children should build on the basic movements that have been developed during infancy. Most infants learn to move their bodies in a natural progression and on their own time. Practice time, with parents' encouragement and praise, develops a child's confidence and self-esteem. Rarely are infants pressured to improve their skills, or judged to use proper forms. Similarly, young children need these reinforcements of encouragement and praise when involved in their physical education classes in school. Above all, I want to encourage many opportunities to practice the basic locomotor skills, concepts, and exercises developed in infancy. Climbing, crawling, running, turning, moving safely with spatial awareness (over, under, through, around, in, out), balancing on body parts, ball skills, game play, and safety, to name a few, should all be reinforced and practiced with repetition. In addition, a quality physical education program will strengthen children's autonomic nerve systems and enhance the five senses. I want young children to value exercise and play in the open air, promoting good health and body function through their positive experiences.

- Introduce and practice as many various movements and exercises as possible.
- Limit exercises not commonly practiced in young children's lives to avoid injury.
- Exercise to improve inverse sense, rotary sense, rhythmic skills, flexibility, and endurance.
- Encourage outdoor activities, climbing mountains, jumping over a brook, enjoying the nature.
- Exercise with an awareness of safety, to avoid dangerous situations.
- Exercise to develop and support a positive self image.
- Practice tag games, chase and evade games, appropriate for young children.
- Exercise dance and rhythms for self expression.
- Develop manipulative skills like jumping rope or ball skills later.
- Introduce exercise on large equipment like gymnastics apparatus.

## 6. Points to keep in mind when instructing physical education of young children

(1) Before working with young children, prepare a proper space that will be safe for the activity. Establish safety rules and review them with everyone. Teach

children how to play safely, be aware of their surroundings, and avoid injury to self or others. Check the equipment for damage and point out any danger if necessary. Check to see if all students are properly dressed. Reassure that the children will be safe.

(2) Avoid forcing young children who may be afraid or unwilling. Encourage students to try if they want to. Give praise for efforts, even if they struggle.

(3) The teacher should use clear speech and plain language to attract the interests of the children. In addition, they should look to see the eyes of the children when speaking.

(4) When a leader demonstrates movement to children, expressing enthusiasm is important. Children will feel your excitement and want to try it themselves. Do not demonstrate the wrong form or bad habits which the children might do. The demonstration should only show proper form with correct movements.

(5) Teachers should work with a smile and create a pleasant atmosphere. It is important for a child to feel happiness, pleasure, and satisfaction. A good physical education teacher strives to share their love of movement and being active, and instill the same fun and pleasure to the children.

(6) It is important to help children recognize the physical size and strength of adults. Children will understand their potential to grow up strong and healthy like their teacher. But we should be careful to modify our power when demonstrating to young children.
(7) Once the children master the basic movements, start to add concepts such as up and down, turning around, and changing directions.
(8) Give opportunities for a lot of movement so that a body warms up when it is cold.
(9) Increase the degree of difficulty little by little. Sometimes, if it is hard for children, they may experience a moderate feeling of strain. But, it is important, to have new challenges at a certain point.
(10) Encourage children to create their own movements and praise their efforts well. Give children an educational sense of superiority.
(11) It is important for teachers to give advice for success, but it is also important to allow children time to think about a solution on their own.
(12) When children learn new concepts, instructors may need to physically move the child's body into proper form, so it will be easier for them to learn and understand the movements.

(13) It is important to be positive when speaking to children who are working hard. Encourage children to do their best and praise them well. Then the children will be motivated and find connection and confidence in their hard work.
(14) If schools have a limited budget, old or used materials can still be good teaching materials. Children can create pleasant exercise and play experiences with fun, imaginative ideas for use.

## 7. The instruction method of the physical education program

At first, assess the children to determine their strengths and weaknesses. Next, evaluate the needs of the students, to start developing the physical education curriculum. Note the similarities and differences between students when reflecting on abilities, personalities, and experiences. Differentiate instruction methods and expectations for individuals so that the instruction meets the needs of each individual student. Regular ongoing assessment is important to ensure all students needs are being met.

Methods of the instruction

① Direct instruction from the leader. Contents, including the sense of values, are taught from the leader directly. Particularly, there are many rules to establish for all students to ensure their safety when participating. Keep rules clear and easy for children to understand so that the children will be successful and safe.

② Creative thinking and imagination for child development. Occasionally, children will make mistakes during class, or may perform movements incorrectly. When an undesirable action occurs, the teacher should assess the developmental level of the student to determine how much to correct the mistake. Children learn in many different ways. Allow young children to learn from their own experiences first, without correction from the instructor, may be more appropriate for their educational development. Sometimes the instructor may only need to encourage the student to keep trying, without correcting the mistake. A child's self esteem is less likely to be negatively affected in this form of instruction.

Initially, the instructor will teach the students the desired actions to be performed, with clear description and demonstration. As the students react to the instructions, the teacher should identify the students who are following the instructions properly, and point them out to the class as an example by saying, "There is a student who is sitting down properly to hear a story." This positive reinforcement instruction method provides learning opportunities for the other children, who see the student performing the desired action.

The instructor should not point out mistakes directly, but show a desirable method for the undesirable action, by using the euphemistic method. When time is limited, an activity to be hurried up as euphemistic instructions, "the girl has me already"; "10, 9, 8, 7"...... The expression that "You were early" is used. In addition, non-verbal instruction of the leader includes a method to show in an expression and a manner.

Children find sense of values from verbal expressions and the manner of the leader when demonstrating, to judge the good or bad. For children, a favorite leader sympathizes, and makes connections, to develop an activity more indirectly. When the instructor addresses the undesirable action, the instructor should consider that students learn best when they are shown in a proper manner, as well as with descriptive words. In other words, children respond to both verbal, and nonverbal cues from the leader, as they assess student performance. Particularly, you must not forget, "existence in itself of the leader rouses the attention of the children." Existence in itself of the leader affects the activity of the children. In other words, the children are interested in the activity simply because they want to perform it like their teacher. Having an intentionally positive tone, when assessing the children about the activity, will lead to greater success.

## 8. End

In conclusion, I believe it is very important to help ensure that each young child succeeds, and the leader of the physical education of young children must use a wide variety of instruction techniques, including modeling and demonstration. Furthermore, instructors should tie the positive experiences of success to new learning experiences to encourage.

These are my thoughts about physical education for young children, that I have outlined here. I hope teachers and researchers will work together so that children's mind and body are healthy together, and children of the world will realize the health benefits of exercise. I call on the thoughtful physical education leaders and researchers of all the countries of the world, to cooperate and start to work together, because this work can not be done alone.

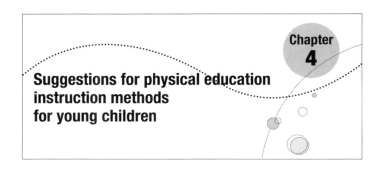

# Chapter 4
## Suggestions for physical education instruction methods for young children

Having considered noteworthy points on physical education guidance for young children, I would like to make suggestions to contribute towards the development of early childhood physical education guidelines. These are noteworthy points to keep in mind when guiding and teaching exercises to young children.

Noteworthy points on physical education instructions for young children

### 1. Noteworthy points at the introductory scene

#### (1) Safe environmental setting

Ensure safety by securing sufficient space and check whether people or things around the young children may be hit during the exercise. Also, let's discuss ground rules or conventions on safety before starting. If a child's clothing is not in order, then only get started after the clothing is properly set. Teaching contents and methods are to be changed according to whether the location of instruction is indoors or outdoors and whether the area is large or small. Consideration for crisis management is also necessary. If indoors, take note of the position of glass and furniture. If outdoors, be aware of hazards leading to falls, including holes and gaps. Be sure that dust, and the like of it, is not particularly a concern. Remove dangerous items prior to starting.

## (2) Clothing

Clothing during exercise should ① allow easy movement, ② be not too thick, ③ include a cap or hat if outdoors, ④ have shoes properly worn and not just be slipping in at the heels, and finally, ⑤ if exercising with exercise mat or equipment, please ensure that long hair is properly secured with hairpin or hair bands on the head.

Please do not forget that the instructor/teacher himself/herself should pay proper attention to his/her own appearance. If the teacher tells the children to tuck their shirts into their pants, but he himself leaves his shirt untucked due to fashion, this will not be a good example. Guys should be reminded not to wear socks on a slippery floor, and should be careful. If the teacher himself slips and falls, he may be injured. And assistance from the children can be hazardous, and first of all should not be considered. Therefore, it is of foremost importance for the teacher to consciously become a model for the children.

In addition, the teacher should help to remove watches from wrists and accessories from the faces and bodies of the children, and instruct them to do so. Attention should be paid regarding the whistle hanging round the teacher's neck, ensuring that its string does not end up winding around a child. Hooded clothing hinders vision and movement, and should be avoided. It is also important for the teacher to cut nails so that they do not scratch or hurt a child's face or body.

### (3) Teacher's standing position

When teaching outdoors, it is necessary to pay attention to the position of the sun and the direction of the wind. If the teacher's standing position is where the sunlight or wind directly hits the front of the children listening to the instruction, the children will be dazzled, cold, and lose concentration. Let children try to be positioned with the sun and the wind behind them. Also, if there are other groups of children who may enjoy playing in front of the children who are in a session, or there may be the coming and going of cars that enter their eyes, the attention of the children are transferred and the concentration is deprived. Therefore, decide on a standing position where there are no people or things taking attention away at the front of children. In particular, when teaching young children, it is good to give a clear standing position, that is, a position where the teacher stands at the time of gathering, to make it easy to understand and secure. When the teacher's voice is issued, it becomes easier for children to predict that the teacher will be in this particular direction, which will make gathering the group easier and make time more efficient.

### (4) Formation

When giving guidance and instructions to children, the better formation to gather them in is the horizontal long formation. When the children gather in this landscape orientation, your voice will reach them easily even if the distance is vast. When the children have easier eye contacts with the instructor, the concentration of the children can be enhanced. On the other hand, if you gather the children in a long vertical line in front of you, your voice will have difficulty reaching the children at the back in a distance, and movement is also less visible. Also, the nuances of the teacher will not be felt by the children. What is critical is to form a formation that allows all members of the children's group to be within the view of the teacher, regardless of the formation. If you are out of the field of view, even if the distance is close, it is difficult for the children to see the teacher, and the children cannot concentrate.

### (5) Alignment distance to children

When the children are called to gather, the children will run towards the teacher, each one trying to be at the front, with the mindset of "I want to be number one", or "I want to stick with my favorite teacher". In this situation, if the teacher does not make enough space behind himself when he calls out to the children, for instance if he stands with his back to the wall, he will have no room to adjust his position in response to the children.

Therefore, when gathering the children, the teacher should stand a little in front of his final intended position to accept the children. After a while, he should try to keep a certain distance from the children by taking a few steps behind. In this way, by taking a moderate distance from the children, movement is easy to show, eyes are easy to meet with the children, and it becomes easier to teach with clarity.

It is important for children to form habits with easy-to-understand contents: keep the place to meet at the start as also the same place to meet at the end. By ensuring that the consistent place is used from beginning and end as the spot for explanation, the atmosphere will be kept calm. When arranging the formation, it is a good idea to concentrate on maintaining the distance between the children in front and the back after arranging and taking the appropriate distance interval between the children on the left and right in the row. If you line up each child in a way that neighbors cannot reach each other, it will become easier to concentrate on just taking the distance in front and behind, and then you will be able to line up quickly.

## (6) Warm-up

We call the preparatory movement "warming up" in English. In other words, it is to raise the body temperature, move the whole body, improve the blood circulation of the muscles, and smoothen the energy supply. It is to bring about the state of the body that improves exercise efficiency, so it will be a condition that avoids injury and enhances accident prevention. Move the body parts far from the heart, move the whole body gradually, and let's expand the range of motion of the joint. When doing it face-to-face, it is important to be conscious of the opposition always, such as left and right, up and down, in the direction of movement. Also, if you run clockwise, incorporating the movement in the opposite direction, such as running around anti-clockwise which leads to better balanced development. It also works effectively on the accumulation and spreading out of teaching content.

(7) Grouping

The same group should be maintained when playing with snow and skiing. In an emergency, at least two teachers must be secured for each group with one person looking after the children and the other person turning around for communication.

## 2. Noteworthy points at the development scene

### (1) Manner of speaking

Let the teacher get the interests of the children with easy-to-understand phrases. Look into the children's eyes when talking. In the case of children aged 1 to 2, it is difficult to communicate in words, so it is a good way to promote understanding by instructing while moving at the same time or showing demonstration.

### (2) Consideration for the fearsome children

Avoid using excessive force on a child who is afraid. Also, even there are things that a child cannot do despite pushing and trying hard, offer abundant praise. Even if all that can be done is just by sitting or watching the guidance nearby, let's try to offer words of encouragement for that effort.

### (3) Momentum

When it is cold, let the body warms up by moving the body more. If the teacher's talk is long, the body of the children will be cold, it will lead to injury and cannot offer the opportunity to practice motor activity skills well. For instance, if the assignment is difficult, and the passageway is narrow, there are no courses to choose, If the number of people assigned is too large or the equipment is small, the waiting time becomes long and the exercise amount drastically decreases. Within a limited time, it is necessary to reduce latency and make it possible to move efficiently and to secure momentum.

### (4) Assistance

When a child does not understand, you can teach by specifically moving the child's body or touching it, then the movement will become easy-to-understand. It is also important for children to feel the size and strength of adults who will assist and help them. When children realize the strength and dependability of adults' power, they are more reliable and reliably involved. But please moderate the power as well.

### (5) Mastering skills

It is easiest to show movement with children of lower ages than to explain by words. When the teacher shows a movement to the children, it is important to express it clearly, being big and energetic. Then, the feelings of trying will come to the children. However, children also imitate the bad habits of adults. Movement shown as an example must be good and firm. In particular, it is important to stretch firmly and bend it enough when bending. Movement is easy, and things that can move the body to the limits are good. From time to time, let's change the direction by moving the body up and down or turning. Since motivation and confidence are necessary, I usually praise children with exaggeration. When it comes to a 4-year-old child,

Chapter 4  43

it is important not to praise only but to explain what is good and what is wrong. When children are five years old, they will be able to act for themselves, so they need to be watched over. By leaving enough degree of autonomy, they also acquire a sense of responsibility, so you need to give them good hints on how to act.

### (6) Sustained concentration

The time duration that young children can concentrate is not long. As a guide, a lesson can often be up to one hour long, while the attention span can range from 30 minutes, but it is also influenced by the child's age, the weather and the season. Let's make the first event of activities for around 10 to 15 minutes. Since long lasting (attention) is impossible, we are required to promote (attention) while changing contents in a short time. It is sometimes desirable to make the tasks more difficult, make the tasks with moderate tension, to motivate the children to move. It is important in terms of focusing on freshness.

The volume of voice is important to attract children to teachers and to keep them focused. In addition to attracting with a loud voice, there is also a way to make the voice small, dare to say "what did you say?" to make the children interested and concentrated.

## (7) The making of a pleasant atmosphere

It is a big point to make children feel "fun" by acting with smiles and creating a fun atmosphere. Also, it is important for teachers to work together to enjoy activities from the bottom of their hearts and feel empathy with the fun and enjoyment of the activities. When the teachers themselves face each other with a delightful and bright expression, the facial expressions of the children will also become brighter. In order to make children feel tense, it is also necessary to have techniques in which teachers change their facial expressions. However, try not to make facial expressions that would make children afraid.

## (8) Feeling of satisfaction

We will move step by step from gentle to difficult things. For young children, if you proceed with a small step, the feeling of "I understood" and "I made it" will lead to satisfaction. Also, we need ingenuity not to let children wait too much. Let's not let children wait psychologically by exercising ingenuity, such as how to arrange children and the position of equipment. It is necessary to observe how the children are playing with tools, not to be caught in the established concept, but to have flexible in thinking from all angles in order to make children feel satisfied.

## (9) Stirring up motivation

If you find good movements that lead to children's devised movements and physical fitness, the teacher can highly praise the movement and give educational superiority to the child. It is important for the teacher to respond fully to the child trying hard. If children are doing well or doing their best, and are devising, you should praise that highly. Then, children will motivate themselves and lead to self-confidence by praise.

Depending on age, the number of people in the group to recommend differs, but if children are over 4 years old, a group of 3 to 4 people to cooperate and to make them conscious of the team is good. If you want children to understand rules and regulations of the activities, it would be better to group up to no more than 10 people.

## (10) Fostering independence, spontaneity and creativity

It is important to give advice on how to do it well, but it is also important to give time and make the children think about solutions. The point is that you need to be careful not to teach your answers too quickly. In order to raise an independent child, I would like you to engage in such a way that you do not give too many answers, let the children think about it and find the answers. Relationships with children who refuse to (blindly) concede to adults and admit it admirably will nurture the independence in children.

In addition, it is important to inform children that it is a pleasant exercise and play even if you use an apparatus and recycled (waste) materials. Day by day, the teacher needs to make efforts to devise the kinds of handmade tools and playthings that can be created using something close to us.

### (11) Response to danger

Always let the children know about how to use, as well as how to safely use the tools and equipment. It is essential to ensure safe exercises to learn the shape, weight of tools, instruments and knowledge about them to ensure safe exercises.

When paying attention to a child who has done a dangerous bad thing, it is not a good way to reprimand with the question of "why do such a thing?", but to tell and stress the reason why such a thing cannot be done or the importance of what should not be done. In early childhood, it is necessary to understand that the head is large and the center of gravity is high. Therefore, planning and guidance with the features of the child's body in mind are required, with attention that the head is bigger and children easily fall down.

### (12) Competition

In competitive exercise, do not just compare with others, but let's make it challenging for oneself. For example, I would like to value the child's intrinsic motivation, such as jumping more times, running faster or jumping farther compared to last time. Relay style exercise places an emphasis on victory or defeat, and it seems to be exciting at first sight. However, if one loses, avoid pursuing the cause and making it a personal attack. Consideration is necessary to equalize the number of people and the proportion of males and females when playing relay activities.

## 3. Ending scene

### (1) Cooling down exercise

Let the children relax the muscle tension used in the main movement, arrange the breathing of the children, and let the mind and the body relax. Try to reduce the accumulation of children's fatigue so that the next activity can proceed smoothly. Especially, in terms of the body, it restores the softness of the muscles which smoothly moves after the former straining. Also, let's ensure the softness of the body by bending and stretching the body in various directions. Even if children say "do not want to do it because we are tired", you do need a cool down exercise. Cool down exercises make children securely handle the organizing movement and can enhance the physical ability with springs that can create movement from various directions. Let's make it a habit.

### (2) Clearing

After using various tools and playthings, the children should have a habit of cleaning up by themselves. The leader should clean up things that are heavy weight, dangerous things and things that are difficult to store in warehouses or equipment boxes, etc. However, for children, items such as balls, cones, mats, tires, etc is manageable. It is possible for children to cooperate with each other and carry them together under the supervision of the leaders who ascertain what they can safely carry.

Also, as one of the teaching techniques, it is also a way to finish the packing and disposal as a last sensation of game.

## (3) Summary of the activity

Let the children aim to reflect and evaluate the aims planned by the teacher in easy-to-understand words. The teacher acknowledges the children's effort, devised ideas and good moves. On the contrary, the teacher will also listen to what children did not do well; let's finish with tips on how to improve.

## (4) Security after the exercise and hygiene

During the exercise, the teacher should remember the fallen children, and the children who scraped their knees, etc., After confirming the injury, check the condition of the injury again. Then, the teacher will take actions and measures such as allowance and necessary observations according to the state of the child.

Also, the teacher should instructs children to wash hands, gargle, wipe off sweat. Let's make these a habit. When it is hot, let the children remember to wipe off sweat thoroughly and change the clothes. While taking care of these concerns, enjoy exercising with children and shed a good sweat. Teachers and leaders should give their children a lot of wonderful memories to bring back home.

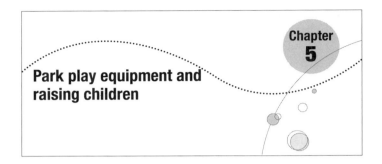

# Park play equipment and raising children

## Introduction

The current trend in park play equipment in recent years has been to actively introduce healthy playthings as a means to improve the health of public park participants. Park play equipment that can easily move the body while remaining fun can also be used as a training tool for health promotion. While enjoying the feeling of playful free play, you can move the body vigorously, It helps eliminate daily exercise shortage and promotes physical fitness. If excellent park equipment is available, you can enjoy the ease and pleasure of using it. In addition, families can enjoy it and they can become healthy while playing too.

In this article, I will focus on park equipment and

children's health. I would like to promote my idea to support the growth of children. Specifically, we have introduced health management problems that children in recent years have experienced and analyzed the significance and role of "park play equipment", and its effectiveness for improving problems, what is the best method of utilization and the best way to improve park playground equipment and notes on its use.

## 1. Health management problems experienced by children in recent years

### (1) Negative influence on children by pursuing an adult nightlife

In recent years, children are caught-up in the night life of adults. When you come out to the city at night, you will see a sign for a bar, "Eat, Drink, Enjoy (Relax)!", "Completion of Private Room with Kids Space". It seems fun, but children are being taken by their parents to those places where I maybe better to add a 'where' before 'I' often see small children entering or leaving at midnight from family restaurants, taverns, convenience stores, karaoke boxes, etc. I've heard: "It's okay, because the child is fine.", "Because the children are having fun.", "Because the night is the time of contact between the father and the child.", "Because the child says he is not sleepy yet". The number of families who are letting their children stay up late is increasing. Currently, some children tend to be "late to bed, getting up late, and going to bed stuffed!"

Meveover, parents have their young children in school gymnasiums that are open for adult health recreation, many adults start enjoying exercise in these exchanges from 9 o'clock to 10 o'clock in the evening. Many children in these situations do not have dinner until after their father or mother finishes their sports. In these situations, children are getting into the night life of adults and are becoming unhealthy. Parents are ignorant to facts about healthy children's life rhythms. Parents need to know that they should not try to have their children match their adult life rhythms. I want to "sound the alarm" to parents to make them aware of this recent trend.

In many cases, children do not have dinner until their parents finish playing their sports. There are situations where children are getting into the night life of adults and are becoming unhealthy, parents do not know how a child's healthy life rhythm should be, they need to know that they cannot match their children's rhythms. The facts need to be brought to the attention of parents with small children. In the night, when children disrupt sleep rhythms, their food does not advance, and it causes scarcity and defecation. As a result, the activity strength in the morning declines and it becomes impossible to move.

Having sleep disorder, absence of taste, lack of exercise, the functions of the brain and the autonomic nervous system which automatically protect the body do not work well, In addition, and the temperature control which is controlled by the autonomic nervous system cannot successfully function as well. After all, the body temperature does not fit in the 36℃ range, it means that the body temperature cannot be adjusted.

What is worrisome is that the children's momentum is drastically decreasing. For example, the number of steps of a 5-year-old child in a nursery school, in the Showa 60 to 62 period, was around 12,000 steps, moving between 9a.m. and 4p.m., but since Heisei 10, it became 5,000 steps, and it drastically declined to about half the exercise amount in the Showa era.

Besides, the use of cars in downtown gardens has become more frequent, so the number of steps in the whole life of the children is decreasing, and the required exercise amount is greatly reduced. When looking at the activities of children, children who are falling cannot keep the balance of their feet, the toes of the feet float when walking on a log or walking the average table top. These occurrences are unthinkable if they walk enough in their lives. Even if they run, they cannot raise their knees securely, so they rub their feet on the ground and hook it. Moreover, their hands are always stopping, not helping in their movement.

## (2) Negative impact of excessive media contact on children

Looking at the playgrounds for young children after kindergarten, the first place is inside the house, 85% of the first graders and 75% of the third graders are in the house, even primary school students are staying indoors. The majority of the play for toddler boys is TV/video, and for toddler girls, drawing is No.1. When you look at the first grade, both boys and girls are TV/video. And for third graders, the boys are playing video games and the girls are using TV/video.

TV/video viewing and video games are objective activities that do not move the body in the house. 3 to 5 o'clock in the afternoon after school, the body temperature is rising at a great pace. Not only are the children not fully using the body, but also opportunities for learning from interpersonal relationships are lost. In other words, even after returning from the kindergarten or school, the children now work individually and do not have enough interaction with other people. When static play is employed by children, TV, video, smartphone, and game equipment increases during leisure time, In this way, the heart, lungs and the whole body are not strengthened and may even cause physical strength reduction (static playing generation). In addition, since they stare at the screen (flat screen) and focus on one point, the ability to recognize the depth, positional relationship and sense of distance of the activity environment become immature, spatial cognitive ability and safety ability do not develop as required (screen generation). So, there are many important reasons to get children in contact with "actual" people.

Even if they say "I am exercising", since they are specialized in a single sports from a young age, they do not experience diverse movements, children who do not have basic motor skills in a wellbalanced state, (There is also a concern about the existence of biased generations). In this way, excessive media contact also threatens the growth of children in the process of development, such as having insufficient physical strength and lower communication ability.

Under such circumstances, as a response to children being barraged by the media environment in the society, parents should start employing a "No TV Day" or "No TV Challenge" to make a day for not touching television, video, video games, etc. For a certain period, all electronic activities such as "out media" that breaks contact with images and challenges something else, a call is made to break off excessive media contact by children. However, simply focusing on devising methods of media usage will not fundamentally solve the problem. In other words, from the early childhood years, children must enjoy the pleasures of exercises involving people, not to be overrun by the draw of television, video, games and so on. However, it cannot be done without parental guidance that needs to include a variety of exercise experiences to get children in shape. We need to devote ourselves to efforts and guidance so that positive memories of one frame of guidance will be an exciting experience that remains in the minds of children. From children, "Oh, it was fun, I want to do more" "I want to do it again tomorrow", parents must provide guidance that will render positive impressed reactions so that the children will want to come back. I am painfully promoting the necessity of teaching parents to actively employ the minds of children through movement.

In addition to teaching methods, making safe environments where exercise can be accomplished is extremely important for supporting children. Going to a familiar park in leisure time, playing with playground equipment in the park, and experiencing the fun of playing in the park not only contribute positively to a child's health and memories, but also help inprove the night rhythms. These greatly contribute to solving sleep-type problems associated with exercise shortages. For the purpose of experiencing healthy play and exercise, I would like to emphasize the essentiality of "park play" and its positive experience to a child's fitness experience.

## 2. How to increase the work of children's brain and autonomic nerves

In order to ensure that the brains and the autonomic nerves of children work properly, first of all, it is necessary to arouse the awareness of the adults who monitor the basic lifestyle habits of their children. They are in charge of scheduling exercise environments in which children can actually move their bodies.

It is necessary for adults to seriously work on making time for daily exercise for their children. In order to enhance the functionality of children's brains and autonomic nervous system, I recommend the following three practices.

① Make children adaptable and responsive to various environmental temperatures through outdoor activities, not inside the house.
② Have a solid experience of "exercise involving people" that moves and responds actively in a safe playing place such as in a park.
③ Through exercise (muscle activity), the blood circulation improves, heat is generated (the body temperature is raised), perspiration is dissipated, heat is released (the body temperature is decreased and the reguldting functions of the body temperature, become activated). If you provide concrete examples of exercise, you can enjoy "fun and active" collective play such as tag and rolling dodgeball, these activities put loads on the body naturally through the play games mentioned above. Using physical strength, movement skill and activities using "fixed playground play in the park" will be extremely effective. These activities will improve the functions of the cerebrum and the autonomic nervous system, and lead to the enhancement of physical strength

naturally.

In other words, during the day, when the sun is out, children should play by moving the body and exercising. This will promote hunger in children, then after a quick dinner, children become be tired and go to bed early. A non-adult sleep rhythm will allow children to get up early, eat a good breakfast and start their day energized and earlier. Since there is time to eat a scheduled breakfast, energy is gained and the body temperature is raised further, then daytime activities and exercise can be started, physical strength also promotes increasing good circulation naturally.

## 3. Significance and role of park play equipment

Among the exercise equipment installed in the park, fixed playground equipment, includes climbing, tools, crosses, ladders, and slides, so the children can enjoy the benefits of actively moving the body. Through playing with the equipment, children will nurture their mental and physical development, social and moral skills, such as the development of cooperation skills. Cooperation and concession with friends, intellectual development to devise ways of playing, together with the danger prediction ability and safety will allow children to develop these abilities. In other words, the park playground is an important life-stage that promotes the growth and development of children. Overall, the park playground is a playground equipment (facility) made for the purpose of promoting children's health, physical strength, and enriching children's emotions, providing children with safe and sound playing scenes and exercise scenes. As you may know, slide tables, swings, and bows are some examples of the well-known playground facilities.

### (1) Slide stand

The slide, which is a standard equipment in most parks, school gardens, and garden courts, has a simple function, but it is fun for all. By sliding down the slide, children develop the body's ability to adjust, it improves equilibrium and dexterity, and will cultivate the sense of speed and the cognitive ability of space. By sliding down with friends, they can enjoy themselves and compete with others while interacting with other children.

### (2) Swing

The playground swing is familiar to children of many generations. It is not only fun, but it also improves the body's ability to improve the weakening balance which kids have been experiencing in recent years.

### (3) Monkey bars

Not only can it improve the upper body strength, but it can also strengthen the overall muscular strength and nurture the sense of rhythm and endurance. It is a playground apparatus that creates exercise that puts a relatively strong load to the body of children. It is a plaything that works on challenging the spirit of children's "challenge". By hanging on the bars to travel they will increase muscular strength, rhythmic feeling, endurance and instantaneous power, as well as rhythmic feeling of making movement more efficiently.

### (4) Monument playground equipment: dinosaur play equipment

Ancient creatures and dinosaurs that can only be seen in a museum are coming to children's playground. Children can experience exercise safely while playing in the presence of real fossils.

## (5) Tree climbing playground equipment

Dynamic tree climbing can be reproduced. As a plaything, children can experience the climbing of a tree, the fun of climbing up the tree, especially branch-to-branch. For safety, a net is tensioned spirally and it also creates a playing space like a maze. Children inflate their curiosity, climb up branches and start climbing toward the sky. Tree climbing play equipment repeats small challenges as many times as possible, creates play and fosters children's dreams.

Children can experience diverse movements such as climbing, descending, hanging and crawling.

① Tree climbing is an athletic playground item that enables children in their growth years to acquire the "challenge spirit" "exercise ability" and "concentration ability" all at the same time. It is a playground apparatus that makes children feel the fun of climbing to high places and the realistic challenge of tree climbing safely while climbing branches and hanging.
② When they are tired of playing, falling down, the net will change quickly to a hammock and wrap their body gently.
③ Climb the tree and reach the summit, they can feel

the refreshing wind. Also, as an observation facility imitating a natural tree, it is a noticeable landscape different from the ground. It is also a point of wonderful bird watching, they can hear birds' singing as well.

## 4. Ability to be cultivated with park playground equipment

By playing with playthings, children will inprove physical fitness, gain various motor skills and will greatly improve motor abilities. Moreover, from the imagination of children, we may develop different types of play, and sometimes it may be a little frustrating, but I would like you to play a lot while watching. That experience will make children grow more and more. We will introduce 10 physical fitness factors, 4 basic exercise skills, ability to be cultivated during exercise when children play with park playground equipment and exercise.

### (1) 10 physical fitness factors
#### 1) Strength

I express it in kg whether a thing of the power to occur by a line shrinking. That is the line which can show how big the power is by the greatest effort.

## 2) Power

Used in the word "Power", it refers to the ability to generate a momentary exercise by instantaneously exerting force.

## 3) Endurance

The muscular endurance of how long the work can be continued under the load applied to the muscle group, and the long-term exercise of the whole body. The cardiovascular / respiratory endurance of the respiratory and circulatory function that are continuously performed can be broadly divided.

## 4) Coordination

Coordination refers to the ability to combine the motion of two or more parts of the body into one cohesive movement or exercise in response to stimulation from the inside or outside of the body. This plays an important role in learning complex exercises.

## 5) Balance

Use of the word "Balance", it refers to the ability to maintain the body's posture. In the movement of walking, jumping and crossing, it is distinguished between dynamic equilibrium which means the stability of posture and static equilibrium which means stability of the body in a stationary state.

## 6) Agility

It is the ability to quickly move the body, change directions, or respond to stimuli.

## 7) Skillfulness

It is the ability to move the body exactly, accurately quickly and smoothly according to the purpose, with dexterity.

## 8) Flexibility

It is the ability to bend and extend the body in various directions by the softness of the body. With superior flexibility, you can do exercise smoothly and beautifully.

## 9) Rhythm

It is a condition including sound, beat, movement, or unreasonable beautiful continuous motion, related to coordination and efficiency of exercise.

## 10) Speed

It is the speed at which an object moves.

## (2) 4 basic movement skills

In order to foster athletic ability, I would like to suggest 4 essential exercise skills. The first skill requires running, jumping and moving. The second skill requires balances, like a log crawl or walking an average railroad rail crossing. The third skill requires manipulating things like catching a ball. The fourth skill requires moving the body while hanging (static) from the iron bar or monkey bars. For the growth of a child's body it is necessary, that all 4 types of exercise skills are incorporated daily, it is necessary. Movement stimulus that are conscious of the play environment are moving, balancing, manipulating, and not moving. If you are good at a (static) steel bar, but you are not good at moving, you should invite the child to "play tags and bonds" in fun play. It will promote the child's ability to acquire well-balanced movement skills, increase their exercise capacity at the same time.

### 1) Locomotor movement skill

It is a technique to move from one place to another, such as walking, running, crawling, jumping, skipping, swimming and so on.

## 2) Balance skill

It is a skill that keeps posture stable, such as balancing, rail crossing, etc.

## 3) Manipulative movement skill

It is a technique of movement that acts on and manipulates things, such as throwing, kicking, striking and taking.

## 4) Non-locomotor movement skill (static movement skill on the spot)

It is a technique of hanging, pushing and pulling on the spot.

### (3) Ability to grow during exercise

Parents should aim for their children to grow physically during regular exercise with the help of proper park playground equipment.

## 1) Body awareness

It is the ability to understand and recognize the body part (hands, feet, knees, fingers, head, back, etc,) and its movement (muscle movement). It is the ability to figure out how your body moves and how it relates to your posture.

## 2) Spatial awareness

It is the ability to understand your body and the space surrounding it, as well as the direction and position relation (up and down, left and right, high and low, etc.) with your body. Children's physical strength, athletic ability, and physical exercise skill will properly increase if children make effective use of fixed playground equipment safely. In addition to that, it also naturally leads to the prevention of injuries and accidents.

In essence, in order to raise children with strong mind and body, it is important to (1) correctly arrange the children's exercise environment (playthings) and (2) practice appropriate exercises to train the body using these playthings.

## (4) Safety management (basic) of park playground equipment and safe usage

Even if it is a safe plaything, if children use it improperly, injury or accident will occur. It is required to know the safe usage of playground equipment and to teach children to use the equipment properly. Of course, not only for children, but also for teachers at school and teachers of physical education guidance. In essence, all adults involved with children, including fitness leaders, should be very familiar with each piece of sports playground equipment. They should all have knowledge of basic safety management and the useful techniques and skills associated with all playground equipment safety procedures.

Concerning the safety of the playground equipment, first of all, prior to installation, carefully arrange the movement flow of children. The flow line and the play equipment should flow, so that when children hit the merges, their movement does not become extremely clogged with children. It is important that consideration is given to the arrangement and placement so that children can develop fun play safely and smoothly with playground equipment placement.

It is also extremely important to secure the space required for activities (securing safety areas). Note the height that is supposed to be reached when a child falls or jumps off playground equipment. In this space, except for the playground equipment body, there must be no facilities such as lighting lamps, manholes, curbs, or any foreign objects such as stone and glass.

Risks of exciting playthings (predictable danger) will motivate children's desire meet the challenge, and under these circumstances, they will further enhance their physical abilities by doing various play and exercise. However, it is necessary to eliminate unexpected danger "hazards". A hazard is the danger that occurs in places that are not related to the challenging elements of playground equipment. There are two types of hazards: physical hazards and human hazards.

The physical hazard is the danger that there is a problem with inappropriate placement and structure of playground equipment, poor play equipment due to insufficient maintenance and management. Human hazard occurs when there is a problem with the method of using the plaything, such as playfully pressing when playing equipment is pushed together, wearing gloves and shoes with cords that can get tangled easily. These dangers are unpredictable dangers in children's play, and adults such as designers, administrators and playground monitors need to be aware of them beforehand for preventive purposes.

Furthermore, use the playground equipment properly, let's play together. When there is a problem with the playground equipment, in order to be able to use the playground equipment with peace of mind, in addition to inspection by a specialized company, we would like the playground monitor to do frequent inspections. If you are using playthings and feel there is the potential for a problem or an incident, it is important to contact the administrator. Early detection and early response will improve accident prevention, so cooperation from adults is necessary. When screws are loose or abnormal noise occurs, it is important that children are instructed from early childhood to instantly inform adults in the vicinity. In addition, we recommend that you may enclose solid playground equipment with a net.

In addition, it is also necessary to plan to reduce the burden due to injury when falling by using urethane material. Even if it is a safe plaything, if children use it incorrectly, they can get injured.

It is required to know the safe usage of playground equipment and to teach the children. It is an obligation that all people using playground equipment and all people involved with children should know. It is necessary to be strict on this requirement.

For example, ① Always take off hard-soled shoes; ② Take off things that easily get caught like mufflers, long shoestrings, scarfs etc.; ③ Do not leave the front of the coat open; ④ Do not take school backpacks on the playground; ⑤ No string or rope; ⑥ Do not throw objects from above; ⑦ Do not jump off the heights; ⑧ Do not wind string around playground equipment; ⑨ Do not play on wet playground equipment; ⑩ Do not play with broken playground equipment, and tell an adult about the defective equipment.

Finally, in order to use playground equipment safely, daily maintenance is important. Implementation of daily maintenance, and periodic inspection are paramount for a safe playing environment. Furthermore, it is important to ask the expert or playground administrator to repair or improve the structural integrity of the playground equipment in order to make it safe for everyone.

Part 2 Movement Activities

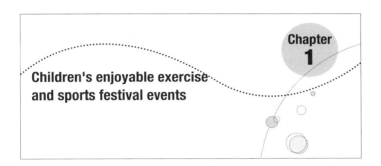

# Chapter 1
## Children's enjoyable exercise and sports festival events

## 1. Warming-up exercise

The warming-up exercise helps relax the tension of the muscles, spread the range of motion of the joints, stimulate the circulation of blood, and increase the body temperature by shaking the hands and the feet, turning the head, and jumping in order to implement the following actions safely and efficiently. Therefore, we will supplement the gymnastics with a large movement that is easy to understand for infants. Especially, it is good to aim at softening the feelings when the infant does not calm down.

In fact, we let infants adjust proper distance and spacing between each other to be able to exercise. The assistance of the warming-up exercise should be done from the back of children as much as possible. The reason is that the lead person becomes invisible once the auxiliary person stands before, and each auxiliary person will lead the infant individually, and it is possible to disturb the voluntary activity of the infant. However, the one-to-one coaching will be very necessary for infants who do not see any movement at all, according to an auxiliary person.

### (1) Warming up

Move every part of the body, and it will increase your body temperature. Begin by fully relaxing the muscles used in the main exercises.

### (2) Changing postures

Kneeling (mother's sitting position), sitting cross-legged (father's sitting position), kneeling on one knee (ninja's sitting position), change quickly according to the instructions.

Mom's style    Dad's style    Ninja style

### (3) Jumping up of Ninja

Swing both arms, and stand up at a dash from the kneeling posture.

### (4) Opening, closing, closing

Move your hands and feet together as you repeat the movements, in a way that your feet open, close, close and your hands horizontally, at your sides.

### (5) Standing up back to back

Sit back to back, arm in arm and with your legs straight. Sound a signal and stand up quickly.

### (6) Mushroom gymnastics

Experience the growth of mushrooms through movements.

## 2. Exercising in pairs

### (1) Clapping

After clapping with both hands and shaking hands, do indicated exercises (pushing each other, pulling each other, etc.).

Chaptar 1  79

face to face and clap    tap (four times)    shake hands (two times)    → exercise

## (2) Rock-paper-scissors: hitting hands

Shake hands with your left hand and play rock-paper-scissors with your right. When you win in rock-paper-scissors, you pat the back of the hand of the opponent shaking hands. The defeated child defenses with the palm of the hand.

wins    loses    loser protects

## (3) Rock-paper-scissors: one circle of the world

If you lose in rock-paper-scissors, you raise one leg and have it with your opponent, hop one lap around the opponent.

wins    loses

### (4) Rock-paper-scissors: drilling through buttock

If you play rock-paper-scissors in pairs and lose, you can drill through the bottom of the winning child's hips. Let's play, rock-paper-scissor of foot, rock-paper-scissors of look, and rock-paper-scissors of body.

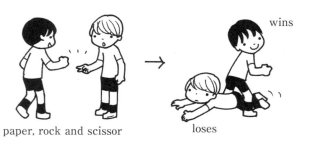

paper, rock and scissor   loses

### (5) Taking tails

Two persons insert towels in the belt of pants and hold each other' hand. Sound a start signal, fetch the towel. The one who took the towel is the winner.

Chaptar 1  *81*

[Note]
· Please do not put a towel on the floor because it is dangerous to step on it and slip over.

## 3. Exercise involving adults and children

### (1) Jumping across feet and going around

① The adult sits down and stretches his/her feet and children jump across his/her feet and go around.

② The adult opens his/her feet little by little. How far children can jump?

③ If possible, can challenge hopping on one foot and jumping backward.

### (2) Jumping and tunneling

① After children jump across the adult's feet, the adult tries to half-rise from the floor to make a tunnel. Children sneak through under the adult's butt (the tunnel).

② It is also fun that the adult blocks children out of the way when children sneak through the tunnel.

③ Not only under the adult's butt, but children can also try to pass through many kinds of tunnels. The adult may try to make a variety of tunnels. (tunnel of press-ups, tunnel of one hand)

tunnel of press-ups        tunnel of one hand

### (3) Jumping and closing feet

① Children stand face to face with the adult, stepping over the adult's feet.
② The adult opens his/her feet on the count of three. Children jump and the adult closes hislher feet.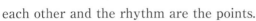
③ Continue the movement, talking to each other. Get along with each other and the rhythm are the points.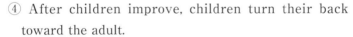
④ After children improve, children turn their back toward the adult.

### (4) Foot race in the air

① Children and the adult sit face to face with each other and stretch their feet toward each other.
② Children keep bending right foot (or left foot) and stretch left foot (or right foot).
③ The adult stretches his/her feet, combines children's bottom of the feet with

his/her bottom of the feet.

④ Keep moving closer together not to move away from each other's feet, and raise the feet to the air to keep this shape.

⑤ Bend and stretch the feet back and forth as if doing the foot race.

### Memo
・It is good to tell to each other "one, two, one, two..." to find the rhythms of the foot race.

## (5) Sumo of crouching down

① Children and the adult crouch down face to face.

② They try not to move their feet position and push each other with their hands close together.

③ The one who is pushed down, placing the body on to the floor or moving the feet, will become the loser.

## (6) Race to step on someone's foot

① Children and the adult face each other and hold hands.
② Children go to step on the adult's foot. If children step on the adult's foot, the adult steps on children's foot in turn.
③ Next, children and the adult try to step on each other's feet. Try to run away not to be stepped on and try to step on each other's foot.

## (7) Patting someone on the butt (using towel)

① The adult holds children's left hand.
② Children go to pat the adult's butt with his/her right hand at a sign of "start".
③ Next, switch the turn and children run away. The adult goes to pat children's butt with his/her right hand.

④ After children get used to play the game, they can try to pat other's butt. Not only trying to pat other's butt, but running away to try not to be patted on his/her own butt.

> **Memo**
> - Adults teach children the easy way to pat by attracting others.
> - Be careful not to pull children's arms suddenly when adults need to pull children's arms.
> - Try to change the holding hands.
> - Expand the scope of action by holding one towel together instead of holding hands with each other after children become used to the game.

### (8) Laying logs

① The adult lays on the back and puts his/her feet up vertically to the floor as if the legs look like a big tree.

② Children drop the big tree (the adult's legs) till it is placed on the floor.

③ It is good that children push and pull from front to back

and from side to side.

④ The adult places both arms tightly on the floor after children become used to the game.

   Memo
  ・Children also pretend as if the massive tree and the adults try to drop it (children's legs) and try to enhance children's abdominal muscles. Adults hold around children's both ankles and drop them slowly. Drop till the children's toes are placed on the floor.

### (9) Push-ups and shaking hands

① Children and the adult face each other and pose push-ups.

② Shake hands while getting their right hands off from the floor. Then, do the same thing by using the left hands.

③ Pull each hand from the pose of push-ups.

④ Jump while getting their right hands off from the floor.

## (10) Wheelbarrow → shaking hands with children who met → somersault

① The adult holds children's feet and children place their hands on the floor and walk.

② After shaking hands with others who met, turn a somersault.

## (11) Pull towel

① Children pull and try to get the towel that the adult holds in his/her legs

② Next, children get a hold of the towel in their legs and the adult pulls.

## 4. Exercise games using wood reuse

### (1) Paper runner (newspaper)

Children open the newspaper, put it in front of their chest, raise both of their hands not to drop it, run and compete with others.

### (2) Making balls of newspaper (newspaper: 2 Sheets)

Children put two sheets of newspapers on both side of his/her feet. Children grab a sheet of newspaper using a hand, keep standing, stretch both hands, and roll the newspapers into balls.

## (3) Catching balls of newspaper (newspaper)

Children open the newspaper, roll the newspaper to wrap flowers, make a megaphone, and a grasping part. Children interfold the parts expanded to strengthen and make gloves. Children catch and play the game by using the gloves and the balls of newspaper that children made.

## (4) Volleyball of a plastic shopping bag (plastic shopping bag)

Put air into a plastic shopping bag, blow up, and tie the bag closed. Play volleyball using the air ball made from the plastic shopping bag.

(5) Catch air balls made from plastic shopping bags
    (plastic shopping bag part 2)

   Two people face each other, each tosses hislher own air ball in the air, run, move, catch the air ball and catch the other's air ball.

(6) Play a game of catching with an apron
    (apron, newspaper)

   Use an apron to catch balls that are made from rolled newspaper.

## (7) Play a game of catching balls with a container (detergent case, milk bottle)

Wash the inside of a used container, cut the bottom of it, keep it upside down like a glove and play a game of catching balls. Make the container's cover as a ball.

## 5. Sports day games

### (1) Torch relay

① Not to drop the ball (torch) that is put on the bottom of an upside-down plastic bottle, run around color cones and return to the start line.

② The next one who receives the torch should run

around the color cones and return to the start line. If children drop the ball (torch), try again from the place where dropped.
③ The team will be the winner which every member returns to the start line.

## (2) Pass through between legs and compete

A child and an adult hold hands together and get off to a start. First, the child passes through between the adult's legs. Next, the adult carries the child on his/her back and return to the start line.

Start line

## (3) Hold hands, fold back and compete

Children run around color cones for folding back, go around the queue, hold hands with the front runner and keep running. Continue the race and finish when everyone returns to the start line.

## (4) Express courier service of kangaroo (game of carrying balls)

Adults hold two balls and children hold one ball. Run together to the point of a color cone for folding back. Adults hold two balls under both arms, receive one ball from children, shoot it in his/her feet and return to the start line. If the adult drops balls, the adult stops at the point and children go to get the ball.

Chaptar 1   95

Children pass it to the adult and continue the game.

### (5) Rolling peanuts balls

① Each team member stands in front of a start line in a row.
② One in each team rolls a ball shaped peanuts, in a hula-hoop forward with a signal of start, run through two color cones, one is a middle-point cone and one is a point of folding back cone, and return to the start line.
③ After going back to the start point, put the peanut-snaped ball in the hula-hoop, touch the next runner's hand and change the turn.
④ Continue the game till the last runner goes back to the start line and put the ball in the hula-hoop.

## (6) Opening legs' race/ laying race/ putting feet up race

This game is a competition with rival teams. Build a team of six children. Members stand in front of the start line in a row. Children move from the last to the front with a sign of a start, cross the start line, and take a big step forward. Step forward at the same time, clap hands. Speak up "yes!" for a sign of clapping hands. At the same time of the signal, the child at the last in the row follows and moves forward, and stride with his/her foot on a child's foot at the head of the row. During this game, run through a point of folding back and return. A team will be a winner whose members step foot inside the start line fast. The races are also fun to lay and put children's body together, and to put feet up, get held by children's both hands next and put children's body together.

Chaptar 1    97

## (7) Laying, setting up, and carrying (obstacle race involving parent and child)

Parents hold children's feet children put their feet up and go to the point where plastic bottles are set (tenpin of bowling). Children lay down the plastic bottles (tenpin of bowling), parents hold children's hands together, go around color cones and go back to the start line. When they return, parents set the fallen plastic bottles (tenpin of bowling), carry children on their back and cross the finish line.

## (8) Carrying shooters by small radius

Three children in one group, they hold a long shooter (a log), go around a color cone for folding back and return to the start line. From the point of folding back, hold between their legs, go around the last of the row and pass the shooter to the next group at the top of the row and relay.

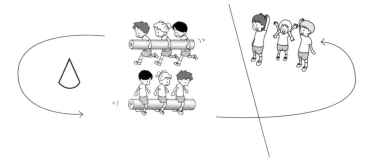

### (9) Safe driving everyday (race blindfold)

Three children in one group, two children from the front put on blindfolds and line in a row. The child at the front of the row holds a hoop and becomes a driver. The child at the back of the row leads the group by voice (verbal instructions).

Chaptar 1  99

## (10) Busy loop (race to pass hula-hoop)

Each team member keeps holding hands together, each child give the large hula-hoop by using the body parts to next child.

The front of the row receives the hula-hoop in hand, runs with it, goes around cones and returns to the back of the row. Continue the game and relay.

## (11) Magic carpet

Two parents put the child on a large bath towel, pull it, carry the child and relay. Runners are two in a team.

## (12) Two people as one and cooperate

① Each team puts hula-hoops in front of the start line, separates into two row and stands in each row.
② The front pair holds hands together with one hand and holds hand gloves (rackets are OK) with another hand.
③ The pair uses the hand gloves with the signal of a start, lifts the ball from the hula-hoop,
④ After they get back to the start point, put the ball in the hula-hoop, give the hand gloves to the next pair.
⑤ Continue the race, till all pairs finish the game.

## (13) Surfing of sea otters

Four sea otters lie face-up in a row, holding the other sea otter's ankles. Other teammates change turns to hold each side of the towel edges two by two, trying to pass the towel under the bodies of the four sea otters.

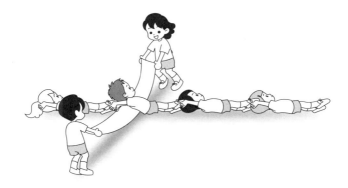

## (14) Cutting waves of flying fish (four flying fish)

Each team has four flying fish lizing face-down in a row. Grab the ankles of the teammates, keep holding and become like a flying fish. Other teammates change turns to hold the large towel two by two, pass it under the flying fish and race. The winner will be the team which folds back fast.

## (15) Taking tails against other teams

Put tails of team colors on each waist. A team will be the winner which gets as many tails as possible from other teams within a certain amount of time. Count each tail which is taken back to their own team territory.

## (16) Go! Go! Hurricane
### (race to carry bars → race to pass hula-hoop)

Two teammates hold each side of the bar, go around the color cone and return, Then, pass the bar under the other teammates; feet and carry the bar to the end of the row. Next, pass the bar above the other teammates' heads and give it to the teammates at the front of the row. Continue the race. Carry it to the line end. And

Chaptar 1  *103*

next, they pass the bar above teammate's head, give it to the teammate at the top in a row and continue the race.

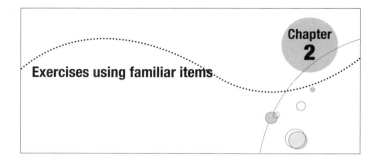

## Chapter 2
### Exercises using familiar items

It is an introduction of exercises that use familiar items, for example, towels, plastic bags in a grocery supermarket, waste materials such as newspapers, plastic bottles as sporting equipment. It is rich in potential and enjoyable change freely to use familiar items. It is easy for children to treat, Besides that, exercises that use the familiar items lead children to know the nature of these items, their intellectual curiosity and inquiring mind can be developed to nurture the ability of expression richly. Primitively ,this is the origin of children's play.

Making use of waste materials and play equipment helps children grow interests and this leads children who are not good at exercise play, to take physical action spontaneously.

## 1. Play to put towels

### Growing ability by play
- Improvement of motor ability of manipulation system(put and hold different parts of the body)
- Improvement of motor ability of transfer system (hold and walk)
- Nurture of bendability and body awareness

### Preparation for play
Face towels (the number of towels should be corresponding to the number of children)

### How to play
① Fold the towel into quarters, put it on the head, back, or stomach, and walk.

② After getting used to the play, try running.

### Memo
- Two hold hands together and play.
- Enjoy the race to relay folding back

## 2. Play to take towels

### Growing ability by play

- Improvement of motor ability of manipulation system (put and hold different parts of the body)
- Nurture of agility, coordination, speed, dexterity, concentration, skills of spatial awareness
- Nurture of sociality, for example, cooperativeness, respect for others and so on.

## Preparation for play

A sport towel (two for one towel) . . . roll the towel vertically long, secure it in some places with rubber bands properly.

Center line (1 line)

Subsidiary line (2 line)

## How to play

① Separate into two teams, put towels on the center line, stand on the subsidiary line, and face each other across the subsidiary lines.

② With the signal of start, run, go to get towels, pull it over to the subsidiary lines and carry. The team which gets a larger number of towels will be the winner.

## Memo

· Pull the towel just like tug-of-war when competing to get towels.

· Decide a winner when no team can carry towels over to subsidiary lines in time.

· In the beginning, prepare some extra towels to make consideration that every child can get towels.

## 3. Catch plastic bags

You may expand the repertoire of play to change plastic bags, for example, expanding, folding, blowing, squeezing and so on,

**Growing ability by play**

· Improvement of motor ability of manipulation system (throw and catch)
· Nurture of dexterity, agility, coordination, bendability, ability of body awareness, and ability of spatial awareness.

**Preparation for play**

Plastic shopping bags of grocery store (the number of bags should be corresponding to the number of children)

**How to play**

① Hold the handle of an expanded plastic bag with one hand, throw

into the air and catch it.
② Catch it by head, back feet and so on.
③ Children try to catch with a variety of poses, such as sternal recumbency, upward, backward and so on, to catch the plastic bags which instructors throw up in the air. After getting used to the play, come running from a distance and catch it.

### Memo
After children get used to the play, form children into pairs to play it.

## 4. Kicking valley of plastic shopping bags

### Growing ability by play
- Improvement of motor ability of manipulation system (kick/ thrust up)
- Nurture of coordination, dexterity, agility, ability of body awareness, and ability of spatial awareness.

### Preparation for play
Plastic shopping bags of grocery store (the number of bags should be corresponding to for the number of children)

### How to play
① Kick expanded plastic bags by feet. After getting used to the play, kick it by right foot and left foot

*110* Part 2 Movement Activities

alternately.

② Thrust it up by palms and try not to drop. After getting used to the play, thrust it up by right hand and left hand alternately.

### Memo

· After getting used to the play, form children into pairs to play it. Compete which pair can thrust it up for the longest time.

## 5. Taking tails

### Growing ability by play

· Improvement of motor ability of manipulation system (take tails of others) and motor ability of transfer system (run quickly)
· Nurture of agility, coordination, speed, ability of body awareness, and ability of spatial awareness..

### Preparation for play

Plastic shopping bags of grocery store (the number of bags should be corresponding to the number of children) . . . fold it widthwise, like a stick-shaped tail,

and put it on the waist.

**How to play**

① After the sign of start, try to take other's tails. Even when tails do not give up but keep taking are taken away, until the sign of end time.

② After the game, instructors ask children the number of tails they took. The winner will be the one who took the largest number of tails from others.

**Memo**

· Let's praise friends who took many tails!

## 6. Race to roll balls by rackets

### Growing ability by play

- Improvement of motor ability of manipulation system (roll balls by rackets)
- Nurture of dexterity, coordination, accommodation ability, concentration, and ability of spatial awareness.

### Preparation for play

Sponge balls (20)

Rackets (2-4)

Color cones (2-4)

### How to play

① Put sponge balls on a line, swing a racket and roll the balls as far as possible.

② Put a color cone at the farthest place where the

rolled ball goes, pick up the ball and return.
③ Play in rotation, each child moves hiolher own color cone to the farthest place where the rolled balls go. The one who rolled most the farthest place will be the winner. If the ball is rolled near the other children's balls, pick up the ball and return.

( **Memo** )
・Hold the grip of the racket.
・At first, hold it by both hands. After getting used to the play, hold it by one hand and play.
・It increases risks of loosing children's grasp on rackets, hitting others around by rackets because of swinging rackets. Be safety-conscious.

## 7. T-ball play: running around circle

How do you play, if you have balls and cones? Put a ball onto a cone, hit the positionally fixed ball by hands and a bat. Put a ball onto T, hit the ball by a bat and exercise just like softball and baseball.

T-ball play during childhood comes to this T-ball is a fascinating exercise play that can enhance children's body adjustability, improve physical strength and nurture creativity and cooperativeness.

### Growing ability through playing

· Coordination, instantaneous force, motor ability of manipulation system, motor ability of transfer system, and ability of spatial awareness.

### Preparation for play

Batting circle(1)/with a diameter of 2m
Cone or batting T(1)
Soft volley ball(1)
Plastic bat (1)
Circle court(1)/circle size with a diameter of 15-20m

### How to play

① Divide two teams to be the same number of members. Decide the turn of offence, defense and batter by rock, scissors and paper.

② The first batter of offence team enters the batting circle and others wait for their batting turn on a bench. Defense team stands out of the circle court at intervals.

③ Batters hit the ball as far as possible, put the bat in the batting circle and run counterclockwise over the circle. Defense members go to catch the ball, and say "stop" while raising the ball by both hands, when they catch it. The batter stops at the place with this signal

④ Next batter hits the ball, the previous batter starts

Chaptar 2  *115*

running along the circle from the place. when a batter goes round the circle and enters the batting circle, the offence team gets a score.
⑤ After every child in the offence team hits a ball one by one, the defense team switches places with the offence team.
⑥ The team which gets more scores will win the game.

**Memo**
· After getting used to the play, play the game by making the circle bigger and increasing the number of games.

- Run in a clockwise way after hitting balls to try to have a balance of children's play.

## 8. T-ball play: ball collectors

### Growing ability through playing
- Coordination, instantaneous force, agility, speed, motor ability of manipulation system, motor ability of transfer system, and ability of spatial awareness.

### Preparation for play
Batting circle (1)

First base circle (1)/ line of fouls to connect lines with a batting circle.

Cones (1)/ putting in a batting circle.

Soft volley balls (6)

Bat (1)

Lines of fouls (2)

### How to play
① Divide two teams to be the same in number of members.

② Decide which team to bat first by each captain's rock, scissors and paper.

③ All team members of the second batting go to the field.

④ The team of the first batting decides the batting

order, enters the batting circle in order of first batter, and hit a ball on a cone as far as possible. After hitting balls, put down the bat, run toward the first base circle, hold a ball in the first base circle and get back to the batting circle.
⑤Children of the defense team catch hit balls. After catching hit balls, hold the balls and run into the batting circle.
⑥ The offence team goes back to the batting circle first and gets a score. If the defense team goes back there faster than the offence team, the offence team cannot get any score.
⑦ After all members of the offence team finish hitting, switch places with the defense team. After all members of both team finish hitting the balls, compete the scores.

Memo

- After children have understood the rules and got used to the play, it is enjoyable to play not only for a first-round match but for some rounds.
- The member of the defense team, who holds a hit ball, not only runs but passes the ball to other members and make it carried to the batting circle.
- It is good to change the rule, to put a ball in a circle after a batter holds a ball and comes back to a bat-

ting circle, and go to catch the ball (one) in a first base circle once again. In this rule, the number of balls, which the offence team members take back to the batting circle faster than the defense team members, becomes scores.
· Enjoy a variation of returning ways to the batting circle, after not only folding back of the batting circle and first base circle, but setting up the second base circle and stepping foot into the second circle.
· Change the size and weight of balls, space of the court and distance between batting circle and first base circle, according to children's levels of sports ability.

*119*

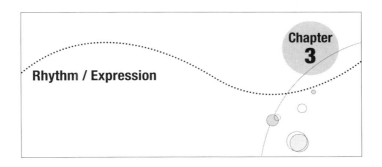

## 1. Circle dance

<Prelude>

Hold hands with each other and make a big circle. Then bend your knees lightly and follow the rhythm.

(first verse) two dogs

① Raise one side of your hands up and show your face through the circle.

Get into a fight

Taro is barking

② The opposite side also does the same way.

③ Fold each other's hands together in front of your chest. In order to draw a circle, swing your arms around once.

"Woof Woof"

Puppy says "bow-wow bow-wow"

repeat ③ ④

④ Fold each other's hands for four times.

Chaptar 3  *121*

"Woof-woof" "Bow-wow" → "Bow-wow" "bow-wow" "Woof"

⑤ Jump lightly with your feet together from left to right alternately.

(example)

<Interlude>
Movements of this part is same as Prelude's.

Number 2,3,4's movement repeats Number 1

Final pause: make a circle freely.

## Purpose

- Each person can use their arms and hands to enjoy the fun of making different forms of circle.
- Using their own bodies to make a circle with the size they like to develop the ability of self-expression.

**Feature**

· Through making circles, the sense of "circle" can be established.

**Considerations during the creative process**

· Some movements such as bending and stretching exercise, jumping, stretching can be used in the warming-up exercise.
· Set a scene that children can express themselves while having fun, and finally can make circles that they like.

| |
|---|
| The name of song: "BOW-WOW" "WOOF" |
| The name of lyricist: SACHIKO MURATA |
| The name of composer: MASAAKI HIRAO |
| The name of arranger: TAKESHI SHIBUYA |
| The name of CD: NHK children with mom super best 16 |
| The original seller: PONY CANYON INC. |

## 2. The choo-choo train in flowerland

<Prelude>

Parents stand behind the children, put their hands on children's shoulders, and keep the four-beat-rhythm.

From the fifth beat, the child rotates his arms around next to the waist, two persons start to move like a train.

*Number 1, From the Anemone station (Stretch right leg)*

① Stand face to face and hold each other's hands, step forward with their right leg, get heel to touch the ground and then put foot back.

*The choo-choo train (tap their hands)*

② After clapping hands one time per person, fold each other's hands twice.

*Primrose street*
*(Stretch left leg)*

① The opposite way of ①
Step forward with your right leg, get heel to touch the ground and then put foot back.

*Running by*
(tap their hands)

Do the same way as ②

*Choo-choo choo-choo beep*

③ Hold each other's hands, the parent becomes the axis and the child circles around in a clockwise direction.
(Not necessarily lift the child up.)
(You can also turn around with the support of armpit)

*Choo-choo choo*

④ Face the front and hold one hand, then jump with both feet, front → back → front → front → front.

&lt;Interlude&gt;
Movements of this part are
same as Prelude's.

Number 2,3,4's movement
repeat Number 1

*Final pose*

The parent turns to the front
of the child, holds the child's
armpit and lifts him or her up.

## Purpose

- By imitating the train, the parent and the child can develop skin-to-skin contact with each other.
- By letting the child move freely, he/she can cultivate the ability of initiative and space recognition.

## Feature

- Through imitation, you can enjoy the fun of the train game.

## Considerations during the creation process

- Try to make the movement of the train follow the rhythm, and lyric, express freely.
- Try to make the movements of stillness and motion

concise and easy to understand.
· In the end, let's incorporate the movement of "high high" so that the child can get satisfaction.

| |
|---|
| The name of song: Chug-chug railway train in a flower world |
| The name of lyricist: JYUNICHI KOBAYASHI |
| The name of composer: YOSHINAO NAKADA |
| The name of arranger: KEIJYU ISHIKAWA |
| The name of CD: 1994 sports festival bodily exercise of anime No,2 |
| The original seller: NIPPON COLUMBIA CO.,LTD. |

Chaptar 3  127

## 3. Warm warm walk walk

&lt;Prelude&gt;

Four people stand in a circle and hold each other's hands, swing hands back and forth following the rhythm.

*Come on*

① Walk two steps in a clockwise direction, then jump.

*Let's go*

Repeat ①

*Warm sun is out*

② Do the opposite way of ① Walk two steps in a counter-clockwise direction, then jump. (two times)

*Come on*

③ Take two steps towards the center hand in hand, then jump

Chaptar 3  *129*

*Let's go*

Take two steps back and jump.

*Walking everywhere*

④ Put hands on the waist, each person jumps around clockwise for four times (rotate 90-degree each time, after four times get back to the beginning position)

<Interlude>

Eight people stand in circle, hold each other's hands and swing hands back and forth while stepping.

Number two, combine with the group next to you, eight people repeat this movement again.

Final Pose

<Interlude>

Everybody stands in circle, holds each other's hands and swings hands back and forth while stepping. Number three, all together repeat the movement.

All the members raise arms up hand in hand, end up by saying 'yay!'

### Purpose

- To extend relationship from parents and children to other people, develop the ability of cooperation and communication.
- By letting children move in different spaces.
- To cultivate the ability of space recognition by letting.

### Feature

- By jumping with the rhythm, moving space, children can enjoy the fun of jumping.
- By interacting with other people, children can experi-

ence the friendliness and intimacy with people.
- Children can also enjoy the fun of the activity by changing the number of people freely.

**Considerations during the creation process**

- It is important to get warm, so we adopt 'jumping' over and over
- By connecting with other people, children can develop the ability of cooperation and expend the circle gradually.

| |
|---|
| The name of song: POKAPOKA TEKUTEKU |
| The name of lyricist: TAKAO HANDA |
| The name of composer: AKIHIRO KOMORI |
| The name of arranger: AKIHIRO KOMORI |
| The name of CD: nursery rhyme best selection ② |
| The original seller: NIPPON COLUMBIA CO.,LTD. |

## 4. Bright red sun

<Prelude>

Two people hold each other's hands and follow the rhythm.

(Number1) *Mr. Sun is rising up*

① Put palms together with each other in front of the chest, move arms around as drawing a circle. When getting back to the former position, put hands together for two times.

*Rising up brightly*

Repeat ①

*Everybody wakes up*

② Hold hands together, get the heel of the left foot to touch the ground diagonally in front of you, then put back. Then right foot also does the same.

*Everybody opens eyes*

③ Reel thread while squatting, then stand up vigorously and open your arms.

*Good morning Mr. sun*

Repeat ①

<Interlude>

Number 2, Repeat the same movement.

Walk around freely hand in hand.

<Interlude>

Number 3, Repeat the same movement.

Walk around backward freely hand in hand.

Chaptar 3   *135*

Final Pose

Skip around hand in hand freely.

Hold each other in arms.

### Purpose
- By walking and skipping, the child can understand the expanse of space.
- By holding hands and hugging with each other, skin-to skin contact can be developed.

### Feature
- By moving around freely, the child can enjoy a sense of space.
- During interlude, you can also take your designed movement freely and extend the activity.

### Considerations during the creation process
- Adopt many simple movements to make it easy to memorize.
- By drawing circle palm to palm, the warmth of the

sun can be expressed.
- By hugging each other, children can keep emotion stable.

| |
|---|
| The name of song: BRIGHT RED SUN |
| The name of lyricist: ETHUKO BUSHIKA |
| The name of composer: AKIHIRO KOMORI |
| The name of arranger: AKIHIRO KOMORI |
| The name of CD: 1994 SPORTS FESTIVAL DUCK SAMBA |
| The original seller: NIPPON COLUMBIA CO.,LTD. |

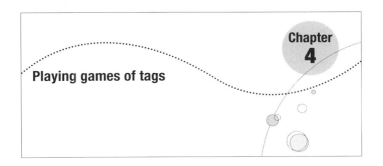

**Playing games of tags**

Chapter 4

## 1. Playing fantastic games of tags can nurture children's mind.

Struggling when you run away, being excited by almost getting caught, a feeling of accomplishment after played . . . children get really excited in an imaginary emergency situation through playing games of tags! Really, nothing is much richer and more amazing experience than this for the brain.

Through emotional ups and downs as emotion control and experience of successes and failures, children enrich their experience of the heart and sharpen their ability to control themselves. It is just a way that children nurture their spirit through playing games.

## 2. Variations are infinity depending on twists and ideas

Though there are a variety of playing games of tags, it can be divided into 4 kinds "one tag", "gathering tags", "increasing tags" and "helping tags". Increase and decrease the number of tags and arrange the rules based on the 4 types noted above. Children can play the games for a long period of time without becoming bored, only changing the level of playing the games based on the level of growth and the situation.

## 3. Step-up of playing games of tags

At first, instructors become tags and make children have a feeling of excitement to run away and achievement. After having understood the rules, children also can be the tags. The exercise volume increases with an increasing number of tags. In addition, the rules should get more complicated and the instructors should familiarize children with playing the games "one tag", "gathering tags", "increasing tags" and "helping tags". on a step-by-step basis.

## 4. Producing "Champions"

　Children can become "Champions" in many ways. Not only children who catch children as tags or run away in the games, but also children who help their fallen-down members, who talk to members cheerfully when they switch the roles, who help instructors and many other children, can also become "Champions". Make the games of tags enjoyable for children to play in a way that everyone can become "Champions".

## 5. "One tag"

### (1) Waving tag

**Purposes**

　Run and stop while judging the situation through playing the game of tag.

**Growing abilities through the activity**

・Agility　・Speed　・Ability of spatial perception
・Motor ability of transfer system

**Rules**

① Draw a line for safety zone over the ground.
② Children sit down in front of the line. At first, an instructor plays the role of a tag and stands toe to toe.

③ The instructor pretends as waves and uses both small waves and big waves for each situation and

catches children only when he/she pretends big waves.

④ Children run all the way to the safety zone and avoid getting caught when the big waves come. Children who get caught become next tags to pretend waves.

**Memo**
・Tell children the basic rules of playing the game of tags. In the game, the tag tries to catch children and children try to run away not to get caught.

## (2) Stepping tag

**Purposes**

Understand the rules and enjoy the change of shadow and Stepping tag game.

**Growing abilities through the activity**

・Speed　・Agility　・Endurance　・Ability of physical cognition　・Ability of spatial perception

・Motor ability of transfer system

**Rules**

① Decide a tag.

② Other children escape when the tag counts ten.

③ Children run away and do not get caught if they are in a place where their shadow hides. However they have to move out from the shadow before the tag finishes counting 10.

④ If the tag steps on the shadow of the child who is running away, which children run away, the child becomes the next tag and the game continues.

(3) Coloring tag

**Purposes**

Understand the rules and enjoy the change of shadow and Stepping tag game.

**Growing abilities through the activity**

・Agility　・Speed　・Endurance
・Ability of spatial awareness
・Motor ability of transfer system

**Rules**

① Decide a tag.

② The tag says a color name and count ten. Children who run away, look for the color which was said and try to touch the color.
③ The tag cannot catch children who are touching the color the tag said. When the tag catches a child who is not touching the color. The tag and the child switch.
④ In the case when everybody is touching the color the tag said, the tag many say a new color.

> **Memo**

· It gets difficult when it is prohibited to touch colors in their own clothes and only one child can touch a place.

### (4)Baby chicks and a cat

**Purposes**

Understand the rules and enjoy the tag game by saving members.

**Growing abilities through the activity**

- Agility · Speed · Endurance
- Ability of spatial awareness
- Motor ability of transfer system

**Rules**

① Decide a cat (a tag). Baby chicks (children who run away) comprise a four-handed group, place their hands upon children's shoulder in front and form a line.

② The cat tries to touch somewhere of the body parts of the chick who is in the last row. A chick who is in the front row tries not to be get touched by the cat,

get in the way of the cat's action, and protect other chicks.

③ After the cat touches the chick in the last row, the chick becomes the next cat and the previous cat goes to the front row of the chick group.

### (5) Dropping the handkerchief game

**Purposes**

Understand the rules and enjoy the "Drop the handkerchief game" that has environmental changes.

**Growing abilities through the activity**

・Agility  ・Speed  ・Ability of physical cognition,
・Ability of spatial awareness  ・Motor ability of transfer system

**Rules**

① Decide a tag to hold a handkerchief. Other children make a circle with everybody, face inward and sit down.
② The tag walks outside the circle and drop the handkerchief behind a child without being noticed.
③ If the tag can go round the circle without being noticed, tap the child's shoulder who has been put the handkerchief behind and switch the tag.
④ If the child notices the handkerchief, he/she holds it and follows after the tag.

⑤ If the child makes up the tag, the tag is the same. The tag changes if the tag sits down to the empty space where the child who has been put the handkerchief by the tag and followed the tag sat down.

## 6. Collecting tags

(1) Collecting tags

**Purposes**

Catch children and appreciate the fun of collecting.

**Growing abilities through the activity**
- Agility  ・Speed  ・Endurance
- Ability of spatial awareness
- Motor ability of transfer system

Chaptar 4  *147*

### Rules

① Set a tag's territory and decide a tag( or some tags).
② While the tag is counting ten, other children run away.
③ Children who get touched by the tag, stay and wait in the tag's territory.
④ If the tag can catch all children in time, the tag wins. If not, other children win.

### Memo

・Make consideration to increase the number of tags and change tags by limiting time to ensure that, not only a few specific children act as the tags for a long time.
・When tags catch children, say "caught!" loudly at the same time while touching children, to avoid troubles of ambiguity that whether the body is touched or not.

(2) Collecting tags' team

**Purposes**

Cooperate in teams and enjoy "Team tag's collecting".

**Growing abilities through the activity**

· Agility  · Speed  · Endurance  · Ability of spatial awareness

· Motor ability of transfer system

**Rules**

① Divide children into two teams (A and B) and set each own territory.

② After touching another team's children, take them to their own territory.

③ A team which is fewer children caught in time wins. Withen limited time, the team which has fewer children caught will win.

> **Memo**

- Show who belongs to which team obviously by their cap colors.
- Find children's good aspects and praise children who can manage to hold on against another team, who can catch many children, or who can run a lot and so on.

## (3) Catching fish

> **Purposes**

Enjoy speed and getting thrilled of going toward a goal without being caught by tags.

> **Growing abilities through the activity**

- Agility ・Speed ・Dexterity
- Ability of spatial awareness
- Motor ability of transfer system

> **Rules**

① Decide a rectangular frame. A tag (one or more) stands at the center and children line in front of a startingline.

② Children start going to the goal with the signal of start, and try not to get touched by the tag. Children can move only in the frame.

③ Children go outside the frame if caught in the middle. A child who is not caught and can cross the finish line, is a winner.

④ Become the next tag when getting caught and continue the game.

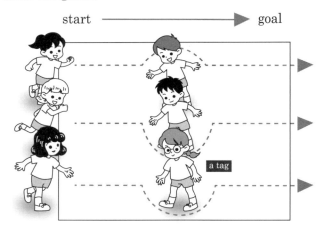

## 7. Increasing tags

### (1) Holding hands tags

**Purposes**

Enjoy "holding hands tags", which requires cooperation to catch children.

**Growing abilities through the activity**

- Speed ・Agility ・Endurance ・Ability of physical cognition ・Ability of spatial awareness
- Motor ability of transfer system

### Rules

① Decide a tag.
② Other children run away while the tag is counting ten.
③ Children who get touched by the tag, hold hand with the tag together and follow other children.
④ Children who do not get caught until the end will become the winners.

### Memo

· Be careful not to fall because of running with holding hands. Especially, children who hold both hands together, are easy to fall over from their head.
· Increasing the number of tags makes the line longer.

Only children at both ends can touch . After getting used to the play, they can use an ingenuity that they impound and touch children who are running away.

### (2) Pulling tags

**Purposes**

Cooperate in teams and enjoy "Pulling tags".

**Growing abilities through the activity**

- Agility  ・Endurance  ・Force of muscle
- Non-motor ability of transfer system
- Motor ability of transfer system

**Rules**

① Divide children into two teams, one team makes a circle, face inward, hold hands (or put their arms around each other's shoulders) and lie face down. Another team becomes the tag.

② The tag team members pull legs of children lying face down and try to pull them from the circle.

③ Children who are pulled, also pull legs of children who are tags and remain.

④ Play the same after switching places and the team which has a largen number of children remaining in time wins.

**Memo**

・At first, decide rules, "not to pull children's clothes",

"not to tickle children" and so on, and tell children clearly.

## 8. Helping tags

The best part of "helping tags" is that the help side and the tag side should think about their own offense and defense strategies. Children run their thoughts full out by themselves, for example, wait until the moment is right, cooperate with some children and open the way. To strengthen their defense, catch for a chance to attack and so on. Children are able to consult with friends and develop the plan, from around four years old. After they play many times, higher level of plans might be born. You can have expectation of children's spreading ideas.

### (1) Freezing tags

**Purposes**

Understand the rules and enjoy "Freezing tags" that requires to help peers.

**Growing abilities through the activity**

· Agility　· Speed　· Endurance　· Ability of physical cognition　· Ability of spatial awareness
· Motor ability of transfer system

**Rules**

① Decide a tag and other children run away.
② Children who are touched by tags, keep their body pause still (freeze).
③ If children who are running away touch (help) children who have become ice, the children who have become ice become able to move again.
④ The game ends when the set time comes or when the tag makes all children become ice

**Memo**

· At first, the instructor becomes the tag, to help children understand the rules, to make the play smooth.

## Arranged plays

◆Banana tags

After being caught, children press their hands together and raise overhead. When other children come to help them by opening up their hands (just like peeling a banana), the caught children become able to move again.

◆Ksitigarbha tags

After being caught, children open both legs with a posture of Ksitigarbha. Children who help, pass through between legs of the Ksitigarbha and the caught children become able to move again.

◆Microwave tags

After being caught, children freeze in the place. When children want to help, they make a pair, and hold hands, with children who froze in the middle between the pair and say "Ching", the sound like a microwave, putting down their arms from up to bottom.

(2) Kick-the-can

**Purposes**

Understand the rules and enjoy a game of tag (hiding tags).

**Growing abilities through the activity**

・Agility  ・Speed  ・Ability of spatial awareness
・Motor ability of transfer system

**Rules**

① Decide a tag and a place to put cans. Other children except the tag kick the can. Children try to hide themselves until the tag returns the can to the original place.

② When the tag has found a child, the tag should shout out the name of the caught child while stepping on the can. Then, the caught child goes to the tag's territory and wait.

③ When the tag leaves away from the can, and the hid-

Chaptar 4  *157*

den children kick the can, children who got caught can run away.

> **Memo**

・Decide a limited area to hide, without making the hiding area too wide.

# Profile of the author
(Prof. Akira MAEHASHI)

### President
### Akira Maehashi (Japan)

Doctor of Medicine
Waseda University, Professor
Japan Society of Leisure and Recreation Studies, Chief Director
Japan Society of Physical Education of Young Children, Chairperson
2005 & 2018 Asian Society of Physical Education of Young Children, Chairperson
International Society of Physical Education of Young Children, Chairperson

### Resume
1978 University of Missouri-Columbia, Graduate School, Master Degree (Education)
1996 Okayama University, Medical School, Doctorate Degree (Medicine)
Kurashiki City College (1987 Lecturer, 1992 Assistant Professor, 2000 Professor)
University of Missouri-Columbia, Visiting Researcher
University of Vermont, Visiting Professor
Taiwan National Sports University, Visiting Professor
Current: 2003 Waseda University, Professor

## Research Works
- Major research on the following aspects: the relationship between fatigue and body temperature of young children; the lifestyle rhythm of toddlers; the parental stress as a result of childcare and child support
- To apply the research findings on well-being, care and education issues of children to make contributions to a better and healthier future for children in Asia
- At the same time, to keep on tackling various young children's lifestyle problems by carrying out nationwide surveys and researches

## Awards
1992 Honorary Citizen Award, Kansas City Missouri U.S.A
1998 Research Award, Japan Society of Research on Early Childhood Care and Education
2002 Special Contribution Award, Japanese Society of Health Education of Children
2008 Best Thesis Award, Japanese Society of Health Education of Children
2008 Well-being Award, Japan Society for Well-being of Nursery-schoolers
2016 Kids Desigss Award (10th), Kids Pesign Council, etc.

## The Administration Staff

**IPEC Chief director**
**Danny Hang (China)**
Beijing Holiday Kids Fitness Edu & Tech Co., Ltd, chairman

**IPEC Public information Committee, Chairperson**
**Toshihito Yamaki (Japan)**
International Association of Physical Education of Young Children, Chairman

**IPEC Plan Committee, Chairperson**
**Yoko Morita (Japan)**
Japan Womens College of Physical Education, Associate Professor

## The Consultant Staff

**Thomas Comet Halley (U.S.A.)**
Lockheed Martin Aeronautics Company, President

**Todd Keenhold (U.S.A.)**
Randolph Elementary School, PE specialist

**Chun-Yuan Fan (Taiwan)**
National Taitung University, Professor & Director of Dept. of PE (Doctor)

**HaoXiao-cen (China)**
Capital University of PE and Sports, Professor (Doctor)

**Lee Jung Sook (Republic of Korea)**
Myongji University, Professor (Ph. D)

## Instructor Training Committee

**Chairperson**
**Noriko Fujita (Japan)**
Life Sports, instructor

**Dashnyam Luvsandamba (Mongolian)**
Academia of Mongolian traditions, President

**Dan Hirose (Japan)**
Childminder school Gakuei Academy, Lecturer

**Xin Lin (China)**
Shanghai ChenLi Sports Technology Co., Ltd., CEO, President

**Shu-Fang Chen (Taiwan)**
National Taitung Univ. Dept. of Early Children Education,Professor

**Eiyu Hironaka (Japan)**
Sono Daini Kindergarten, Teacher

**Stella Wang (China))**
Youth Tree School , President

**Ma Tianxue (China)**
HKB International Ltd. ,Managing director

## Japan Society of Physical Education of Young Children, Professional Instructors

**Kenji Harada (Japan)**
Sendai University, Professor

**Hitoshi Ikeya (Japan)**
Sawada Sports Club, Head Instructor

**Masaru Takashima (Japan)**
Jacpa Corporation, Vice President

**Nobuhito Nagai (Japan)**
Osaka Seikei college, Senior Lecturer

**Hiroko Ishii (Japan)**
Kyoto Notre Dame University, Associate Professor

**Keiko Matsubara (Japan)**
Uekusa Gakuen Junior College, Associate Professor

**Kouichi Koishi (Japan)**
Waseda University (Dr.Maehashi Lob), Teacher

**Yoko Gomi (Japan)**
Waseda University (Dr.Maehashi Lob), Teacher

**Ya-Ting Yu (Taiwan)**
National Taiwan Sport University, Assistant Professor
Waseda University (Dr.Maehashi Lob), Teacher

## Editorial Board

Jacpa Corporation, Manager
Chikano Kato (Japan)
1-7-14 Misono-cho, Kodaira City, Tokyo, 187-0041
Japan

Jacpa Corporation, Staff
Mariko Takata (Japan)
1-7-14 Misono-cho, Kodaira City, Tokyo, 187-0041
Japan

■編著者略歴

前橋　明（まえはし　あきら）
　早稲田大学人間科学学術院 教授／医学博士
　国際幼児体育学会会長
　日本幼児体育学会会長
　インターナショナルすこやかキッズ支援ネットワーク代表
　日本食育学術会議会頭
　日本レジャー・レクリエーション学会理事長・事務局長
　米国ミズーリー大学で修士（教育学）を、岡山大学で博士（医学）を取得。著書に『乳幼児の健康』『幼児体育〜理論と実践〜』『いま、子どもの心とからだが危ない』（大学教育出版）、『あそぶだけ！公園遊具で子どもの体力がグングンのびる！』『0・1・2さいのすこやかねんねのふわふわえほん』（講談社）、『3歳からの今どき「外あそび」育児』（主婦の友社）、『決定版！保育の運動あそび450』（新星出版社）など。
　1998年に日本保育学会研究奨励賞、2002年に日本幼少児健康教育学会功労賞、2008年に日本保育園保健学会保育保健賞を受賞。

# Health and Physical Education of Young Children

2019年11月10日　初版第1刷発行

■編　　　者── 国際幼児体育学会
■編 著 者── 前橋　明
■発 行 者── 佐藤　守
■発 行 所── 株式会社 大学教育出版
　　　　　　〒700-0953　岡山市南区西市855-4
　　　　　　電話（086）244-1268（代）　FAX（086）246-0294
■印刷製本── モリモト印刷（株）
■イラスト── 大森和枝
■Ｄ Ｔ Ｐ── 難波田晃子

Ⓒ Akira Maehashi 2019, Printed in Japan
検印省略　　落丁・乱丁本はお取り替えいたします。
本書のコピー・スキャン・デジタル化等の無断複製は著作権法上での例外を除き禁じられています。本書を代行業者等の第三者に依頼してスキャンやデジタル化することは、たとえ個人や家庭内での利用でも著作権法違反です。

日本音楽著作権協会（出）許諾第190912024-01号
ISBN978-4-86692-050-4